South Asian Mothering

Negotiating Culture, Family and Selfhood

South Asian Mothering

Negotiating Culture, Family and Selfhood

Edited by

Jasjit K. Sangha and Tahira Gonsalves

DEMETER

DEMETER PRESS

Published by:
Demeter Press
c/o Motherhood Initiative for Research and
 Community Involvement (MIRCI)
140 Holland St. West, P.O. 13022
Bradford, ON, L3Z 2Y5
Telephone: 905.775.9089
Email: info@demeterpress.org
Website: www.demeterpress.org

Demeter Press logo based on Skulptur "Demeter" by Maria-Luise Bodirsky
<www.keramik-atelier.bodirsky.edu>

Printed and Bound in Canada

Front cover design: Erik Mohr
Front cover artwork: Seema Kohli "Untitled," 2011, mixed medium on canvas, 60" x 70", <www.seemakholi.com>.

Library and Archives Canada Cataloguing in Publication

 South Asian mothering : negotiating culture, family and
selfhood / edited by Jasjit K. Sangha and Tahira Gonsalves.

Includes bibliographical references.
ISBN 978-1-927335-01-7

1. Motherhood—Social aspects. 2. Mothers—Social conditions.
3. South Asians—Social conditions. I. Gonsalves, Tahira, 1974–
II. Sangha, Jasjit K., 1973–

HQ759.S69 2013   306.874'3089914   C2013-900635-4

For our children,
Simryn, Zeulewan and Safik

Table of Contents

Introduction:
Contextualizing South Asian Motherhood
Jasjit K. Sangha and Tahira Gonsalves
1

RESHAPING, RECLAIMING, RESISTING

From *Parayi* to *Apni*:
Mothers' Love as Resistance
Rachana Johri
17

Lessons of *Izzat*
Mandeep Kaur Mucina
33

Children's Identity Formation in the Sikh Diaspora:
An Exploration of Sikh Mothers' Roles
Tarnjit Kaur
47

The Fires of Transformation
Jasjit K. Sangha
62

South Asian Activist Mothers Speak Out About Politics,
Sexuality, and Health
Jasjit K. Sangha and Tahira Gonsalves
70

MOTHERINGM, MENTAL HEALTH AND WELL-BEING

New Mothers in a New Land:
The First Time Mothering Experiences of Sri Lankan Tamils
Soumia Meiyappan and Lynne Lohfeld
85

South Asian Mothers with Special Needs Children
Satwinder Kaur Bains
101

Mothers and Warriors
Sadia Zaman
111

Mothering the South Asian Mother:
Stories from Midwifery
Manavi Handa
116

Empowering Punjabi Mothers:
A Commentary on Integrated Holistic Counselling
Baldev Mutta
126

COMPLICATING WOMEN'S WORK

The "Sweat and Blood" of Womb Mothers:
Commercial Surrogates Redefining Motherhood in India
Amrita Pande
135

CONTENTS

Perspectives on Work and Family Lives:
Exploring the Lived Experiences of South Asian Immigrant
Mothers Working from Home in Toronto
Srabani Maitra
150

ICONIC MOTHERING, OUTLAW MOTHERING

Selfless to Selfish: Trajectory of "Mother"
from Bollywood's *Mother India* to *Pyar Mein Twist*
Amber Fatima Riaz
165

Baburao Bagul's *Mother*:
A Case of "Outlaw" Dalit Mothering
Mantra Roy
176

Contributor Biographies
186

Acknowledgements
191

Introduction

Contextualizing South Asian Motherhood

JASJIT K. SANGHA AND TAHIRA GONSALVES

A S INDIAN FEMINIST Jasodhara Bagchi asserts, "Motherhood without the mother's selfhood is not complete" (2006: 20). Through this book we delve into a conversation about how South Asian mothers cultivate and express their selfhood, while navigating South Asian cultural norms and values within the social context of their lives. We contemplate how the act of *mothering* can be a source of empowerment despite being entrenched in the patriarchal institution of *motherhood* that places excessive demands, expectations and responsibility on mothers (Rich; O'Reilly 2007). We seek answers to questions such as: How is motherhood socially constructed in South Asian culture and what are the implications of this on mothers? How do South Asian mothers express their agency? How does migration affect South Asian mothers' practice of mothering and their health and well-being? What role do kinship networks play in South Asian mothers' lives? In this way, through a mixture of theory, research and lived experience, the chapters in this edited collection offer insight into the experiences of South Asian mothers and how they negotiate culture, family and selfhood.

To begin, we use the term South Asian with misgivings. Although South Asian is a convenient term that refers to people who have roots in South Asia—i.e., India, Pakistan, Bangladesh, Nepal, Sri Lanka and surrounding areas—it puts a very diverse population of over 1.5 billion people into the same category. It does not capture the heterogeneity of this group of people amongst whom there are differences in language, religion, ethnicity, geography, and cultural practices regionally within South Asia and in the diaspora. As such, this book represents a snapshot of the lives of some South Asian mothers, and is not representative of all South Asian

1

mothers. We are also aware that by highlighting cultural practices that may be deemed to be traditional or "backward" in mainstream Western society we are inadvertently reinforcing stereotypes about South Asian women. It is our hope that readers will question these stereotypes and strive to develop a more nuanced understanding of South Asian culture and how it informs the lives of South Asian mothers.

CULTURE, CONTEXT AND AGENCY

In her edited collection, *Motherhood in India: Glorification Without Empowerment?* Maithreyi Krishnaraj states,

> It is not the fact of mothering that makes women vulnerable, but their social construction, the implications for women flowing from the meaning attached to the idea of motherhood, and the terms and conditions under which it is allowed to express itself. (7)

In South Asian culture, motherhood has historically held significant meaning and women's reproductive abilities have been celebrated, through rituals performed in ancient India, writings in religious texts in Buddhism, Hinduism, Islam and Sikhism, and traditional practices of matriarchy in some communities (Bagchi 2010; Bhattacharji; Krishnaraj 2010b; see also Kaur in this volume). However, along with this reverence came terms and conditions, steeped in patriarchy, that defined how women should mother. Most notably, that women should aspire to motherhood within a heterosexual marriage, and as mothers, they should be sacrificial and devoted to their families (Poonacha).

This historical emphasis on the sanctimoniousness of family life within South Asian culture plays an enduring role in South Asian mothering practices. As researchers have shown, for many South Asian mothers, their identity becomes intertwined with the needs of the family to such an extent that they may often feel a strong sense of duty and obligation, and understand their role as that of providing selfless service to the family while putting their own needs last (Grewal, Bottorff and Hilton). The perception that they need to fulfill this culturally constructed role in order to be a "good mother" is heightened further by gendered assumptions and expectations that are held by their immediate family, extended family and the wider South Asian community. The consequence of this, is that South Asian women are often socialized to perform motherhood in a way that neglects their selfhood. If a South Asian mother oscillates away from this predetermined role, not only is she questioning her own identity, but also her standing within her wider kinship network (Thiagarajan).

However, how this cultural construction of motherhood is deliberated by South Asian mothers is dependent on the particular circumstances within which she mothers and the broader social context that informs those circumstances. As scholars have shown, South Asian mothers' experiences are not just informed by their gender, but through other systems of oppression that intersect with gender such as race, caste, class, sexuality and ability (Bhattacharya; DasGupta and Das Dasgupta; Daudji et al). As well as factors such as hierarchy in the joint family, son preference, religious beliefs, and conflict and/or violence in the home (Bhopal; Sinha; Thiara and Gill). Migration adds another layer of complexity as mothers can face marginalization from mainstream society due to racism, deskilling, isolation and language barriers as well as judgement from within the South Asian community when culturally determined gender roles become equated with South Asian identity and women are measured against these (Kallivayalil; Mehotra).

Therefore, how South Asian mothers interpret culture is not static or fixed, but more fluid, as a multitude of factors shape the framework within which they engage in their mothering practice. The work of Bandana Purkayastha further complicates this analysis, as she refers to the parameters within which South Asian women mother as a "matrix of domination" (30). She states, that within this matrix, social processes that contribute to subordination intersect with other social processes that reinforce power, at times simultaneously (30). For example, a mother may have access to power because of her caste, class and social status yet succumb to restrictions on her mobility and sexuality in order to maintain her *izzat* (honour) (see Johri in this volume). Or a mother may have privilege due to her geographic location after migration, yet face a severe decrease in her standard of living, due to barriers around obtaining paid work (Maitra). While Purkayastha's work illustrates how "constellations of privilege and marginalization" contribute to the diversity of South Asian mothers' experiences, it also explains how the expression of agency by mothers—through the act of mothering—will also be varied depending on the matrix that shapes their lives (14).

Drawing from her work with South Asian mothers, Srabani Maitra surmises that "agency needs to be understood in its full complexities and ambiguities rather than blindly equating it with outright collective defiance or resistance" (48). The chapters in this book tease out this intricacy by showing that expressions of agency by South Asian mothers can take many forms, some of which may not readily be perceived as powerful because they are a subtle disruption of the oppression that mothers might face rather than overt acts. These acts include finding appropriate services for their disabled child after facing stigma from the South Asian community (see Bains in this volume) or growing their child's *kesh* (hair) as a visible marker of their Sikh religion while living in the diaspora (see Kaur in this volume). Despite the differences in how agency is outwardly enacted, it still has significant meaning for the mothers involved. The interplay between subordination and contestation in the lives of South Asian mothers is evident throughout the chapters in this book.

BUILDING DIALOGUE

This edited collection contributes to literature on mothering through four main themes that highlight the nuances of South Asian mothers' experiences. This book discusses how cultural constructions of motherhood, despite being embedded in patriarchy, do not preclude mothers' attempts to assert power or agency. Similar to the distinction between *motherhood* and *mothering* outlined by scholars such as Adrienne Rich, Andrea O'Reilly, Marie Porter and Fiona Joy Green, this book shows how South Asian mothers assert their power through their mothering practice even though cultural practices such as *izzat* (honour), *kanyadaan* (giving away of a virginal bride), caste, or hierarchy within the joint family, may impose limitations on their lives. This book expands our notion of how the impossible ideal of the "good mother" translates into another culture, and the specific ways in which the pressure to fulfill this ideal plays out for South Asian mothers.

The book adds to work by scholars such as bell hooks, Patricia Hill Collins, Kim Anderson, D. Memee Lavell-Harvard and Jeannette Corbiere Lavell and Dorsía Smith Silvia who have attested that mothering has been a site of resistance for mothers of colour who have sought to ameliorate the impact of racialization and subjugation through their mothering practice.

4

Chapters in this book show what this resistance means for South Asian mothers through a discussion of the obstacles experienced by mothers due to: the racial profiling of Muslims post 9/11; being a queer South Asian mother; having a disabled child; being a gestational surrogate; or facing racism and deskilling when trying to enter the labour market. Through these chapters, the book outlines how South Asian mothers push back against attempts to subordinate them or their children.

This book also reveals the enduring nature of culture and how culture "travels" through mothering practices, from South Asia to diasporic communities, contributing to work on mothering and migration by scholars such as Bandana Purkayastha, Usha George and Saira Maiter, Sangeeta R. Gupta, Shamita Das Gupta and Diya Kallivayalil. As these scholars assert, mothers are not passive transmitters of South Asian culture, rather, they play an active role in setting the terms and conditions in which culture is reproduced in the South Asian diaspora. Chapters in this book speak to the process of negotiation that mothers go through after the upheaval caused by migration, when making decisions about which South Asian values to impart on their children, through an exploration of the experiences of: newcomer Tamil mothers; a stepmother in a bi-racial stepfamily; and Sikh mothers.

And lastly, this book expands on work by scholars such as Sukhdev Grewal et al., Sharin Baldwin and Peter Griffiths, and Kate Reed that highlights the need for culturally competent health and social services for South Asian mothers in Western multicultural societies. As these scholars outline, South Asian culture plays a determinant role in shaping South Asian mothers' sense of self and their relationship with their families, and this in turn has a direct effect on how South Asian mothers take care of their own health and well-being. In this book, two chapters written by South Asian service providers address this issue directly through their discussion of providing midwifery services to South Asian women and developing a family counseling model to help alleviate family conflict and violence. As well, a short story provides a real-life example of a South Asian mother's experiences of caring for a very sick child.

Through these four themes that are interwoven throughout the book, we want to build dialogue on the subtleties of culture and dispel myths or stereotypes about how culture influences South Asian women's mothering practices.

OVERVIEW OF THE BOOK

The contributors to this collection reflect a diversity of viewpoints, geographic locations and backgrounds. While most of the authors in this book are academics, we also have contributions from activists and social workers, as well as creative reflections by mothers. We were intentional in our inclusion of voices that are rich in experience yet often overlooked in academic literature. We also sought to include work in this book that would be accessible to multiple audiences by linking theory with practice and validating lived experiences. The fourteen chapters in this book are divided into four sections that represent the main topics that are covered in this book: Reshaping, Reclaiming, Resisting; Mothering, Mental Health and Well-Being; Complicating Women's Work; and Iconic Mothering, Outlaw Mothering.

Reshaping, Reclaiming, Resisting

Within South Asian communities, both in South Asia and in the diaspora, mothers are deemed to be the bearers of culture with the onus of ensuring that children—especially girls—adhere to South Asian cultural norms and values. This responsibility can be restrictive and affect how South Asian mothers interact with their children. However, as the five chapters in this section outline, when mothers are placed in a position of marginality, they rework this position and find power within it by reshaping, reclaiming and resisting cultural expectations that are placed upon them.

In her chapter *"From Parayi to Apni: Mothers' Love as Resistance,"* Rachana Johri explores how cultural concepts and practices such as Shakti (*divine feminine energy*), *kanyadaan* (giving away of a virginal daughter in marriage) and *izzat* (honour) contribute to how womanhood and motherhood is constructed in India. Through her interviews with upper-class Hindu mothers in India, she shows how these women question and resist the cultural socialization that they were subjected to, and in turn, imparted on their daughters.

Mandeep Kaur Mucina's chapter, "*Lessons of* Izzat," elaborates further on the historical and cultural meaning of *izzat* (honour) and how this practice controls and regulates women's mobility and sexuality. Mucina's work reveals how the meaning attached to *izzat* was as relevant for her, living in the South Asian diaspora, as it was for the women in Johri's article who were situated in India. She comments on how, by reclaiming her *izzat* on her own terms, she was able to find strength in this cultural practice.

Tarnjit Kaur's chapter, "*Children's Identity Formation in the Sikh Diaspora: An Exploration of Sikh Mother's Roles*" focuses on how devout Sikh mothers find solace in religion. She examines the decision by Sikh mothers in Britain, Canada and the United States to cultivate a visible Sikh religious identity through maintaining their children's *kesh* (unshorn hair). She explains how this decision is an act of power for the mothers, for whom their religious identity plays a defining role in their mothering practice, despite racism and backlash they may experience on account of this.

The chapter by Jasjit K. Sangha, "*The Fires of Transformation,*" offers another vantage point on how faith can be a source of solace for South Asian mothers. She highlights how, through reclaiming her spirituality, she was able to attain the inspiration she needed to delve more deeply into herself and overcome anger and resentment she experienced as the full-time stepmother to two adolescent stepdaughters in a bi-racial stepfamily.

In the final chapter in this section, "*South Asian Activist Mothers Speak Out About Politics, Sexuality and Health,*" Jasjit K. Sangha and Tahira Gonsalves interview South Asian activist mothers. For these women, resistance is not just in relation to culture and tradition (although that does occur), rather it is in response to attempts to subordinate them due to the public meaning attached to their personal identities as a Muslim mother, a queer mother, and a mother whose children have a rare health condition.

Mothering, Mental Health and Well-being

The mental health and well-being of South Asian mothers living in the diaspora can be affected for many reasons, such as: isolation and poverty related to migration, having a child who is vulnerable due to an illness or disability, or because of conflict and violence in the home. The insularity of the South Asian community as well as pressure to live up to South Asian cultural ideals of motherhood can exacerbate mothers' stress. However, as the authors in this section outline, by expressing their autonomy and accessing relevant support services (which are very limited) South Asian mothers are able to restore their sense of self.

In their chapter, "*New Mothers in a New Land: The First Time Mothering Experiences of Sri Lankan Tamils,*" Soumia Meiyappan and Lynne

Lohfeld show that Tamil newcomer women who are first-time mothers experience significant stress, isolation and sadness as they transition to life in a new country while also learning how to be a mother. They assert that an awareness of the social context of Tamil Mothers is needed by health care providers to ensure that these mothers attain the help they need in the post-partum period.

Satwinder Kaur Bains's chapter, "*South Asian Mothers With Special Needs Children,*" offers another layer to better understand the mental health needs of South Asian mothers by highlighting the stigma attached to having a disabled child in the South Asian community. She shows that while tight-knit kinship networks can isolate mothers who are hesitant to seek help outside the community, mothers who do find appropriate services were buoyed by the support and validation they received and tried to reach out to other South Asian mothers whose child had a disability.

The chapter by Sadia Zaman, "*Mothers and Warriors,*" exemplifies the vulnerability faced by South Asian mothers, through her own account of caring for her very sick child. Zaman describes how, through donning the metaphorical armour, shield and sword of a warrior, she was able to reinvent herself from a grieving mother who feels guilt about her son's health condition to a warrior who becomes a pillar of strength for her son.

Work by Manavi Handa and Baldev Mutta offers innovative solutions to bolster the health and well-being of South Asian mothers who are experiencing challenges in their lives. In her chapter, "*Mothering the South Asian Mother,*" Handa writes about her work as a midwife, providing informed care to newcomer South Asian women who are often living in poverty and lacking proper health insurance due to government regulations. Her work has a significant impact on these mothers by contributing to positive health outcomes for them.

In the final chapter in this section, "*Empowering Punjabi Mothers: A Commentary on Integrated Holistic Counselling,*" Baldev Mutta provides further depth to this discussion of South Asian mothering and mental health through his reflection on the work he is doing at Punjabi Community Health Services. He explains how the cultural socialization of Punjabi mothers puts them at risk of over-extending themselves and being susceptible to abuse. He explains how an integrated holistic counseling model that involves the whole extended family builds the capacity of Punjabi women and slowly changes cultural attitudes.

Complicating Women's Work

Another realm in which South Asian mothers negotiate culture, family and selfhood is that of paid work. As the two chapters in this section show, through their work—in areas such as home-based businesses or commercial gestational surrogacy—South Asian mothers exert their authority within the family due to having access to financial resources. They also contest South Asian interpretations of motherhood through engaging in work that disrupts traditional forms of family, and requires their family to be cognizant of their needs.

The women in Amrita Pande's chapter, "*The 'Sweat and Blood' of Womb Mothers: Commercial Surrogates Redefining Motherhood in India,*" question assumptions about how mothering is defined. Rather than understanding it as being based on biological ties alone, the surrogates regard themselves as the mothers of the children due to the "sweat and blood" of their work and the emotional bond they have with the growing baby. Through their paid work, the surrogates also shift the dynamics within their own families as they have to live separately for the duration of the surrogacy.

Srabani Maitra's chapter, "*Perspectives on Work and Family Lives: Exploring the Lived Experiences of South Asian Immigrant Mothers Working from Home in Toronto,*" outlines how some South Asian mothers chose home-based work, rather than working outside the home in a low paying sector, after they experienced deskilling and discrimination in the Canadian labour market. Instead, they decided to set up home-based businesses so they could care for their children and still leverage power in the family through making a financial contribution that was important to their standard of living.

Iconic Mothering, Outlaw Mothering

The two chapters in this section focus on representations of South Asian mothers in film and literature. While in the first chapter the author explains how the image of the ideal Indian mother has been valorized in Bollywood films over the past 60 years, in the second chapter the author analyzes a contrasting image depicted in a short story, that of a Dalit mother who is seen as subversive for daring to overstep the boundaries of acceptable behavior and conduct for a widowed mother.

In her chapter, "*Selfless to Selfish: Trajectory of 'Mother' from Bollywood's* Mother India *to* Pyar Mein Twist,*" Amber Fatima Riaz explores the complex and layered constructions of mothers in Indian film, from an iconic classic of the 1950s to a contemporary Bollywood film targeting diasporic audiences. Riaz argues that while Bollywood has shifted some of the constructs surrounding motherhood, fundamentally, the ideal of the "good mother" as someone who is sacrificial and puts her children's needs before her own, remains intact.

Mantra Roy's chapter, "*Baburao Bagul's* Mother: *A Case of 'Outlaw' Dalit Mothering*," complicates this notion of what a "good mother" is in South Asian culture, through her textual analysis of a story about a young widowed Dalit mother who dares to engage in "outlaw" mothering by choosing to live independently and express her sexuality. This chapter shows how, although, caste, class, and patriarchy converge to subordinate this mother, she does make an attempt to express her selfhood.

CONCLUDING THOUGHTS

As the chapters in this book have outlined, South Asian cultural constructions of motherhood influence how South Asian mothers understand themselves, their role as mothers, and their relationships with their children. However, *how* culture is embedded in their mothering practice and to *what* extent it shapes or constrains their agency as mothers depends on the intersection of power and subordination in the social context of their lives. Through this multifaceted representation of South Asian mothers, we seek to move beyond conceptions of gender and mothering which silence South Asian mothers because their interpretation of agency and power differs from dominant discourse (Purkayastha 31). Rather, we offer another vantage point through which to examine agency, and how it is expressed by mothers, by going beyond a gender analysis and looking at factors such as race, class, caste, religion and culture.

This book also offers an important perspective on South Asian mothering by exploring the experiences of mothers both in South Asia and the diaspora. This shows the lasting nature of cultural practices and how they continue to hold meaning for mothers despite the crossing of borders and continents. But more importantly, it shows how the migration experience affects South Asian mothers. They must negotiate cultural norms and values as well as their practice of mothering, within a social milieu that undermines their identities, cultural practices, religion, etc.

and subjects them to stereotypes that homogenize their experiences and strip them of their voice.

While this book opens up dialogue on South Asian mothering, further research is needed to explore areas such as: how second generation South Asian mothers in the diaspora navigate South Asian cultural ideologies of motherhood; how globalization, economic growth in South Asia and transnationality affects South Asian mothers; how online conversations occurring through social media, blogs and online magazines such as *masalamommas* are influencing or changing South Asian mothering practices; and how increased public consciousness about violence against women within South Asia will affect South Asian cultural constructions of womanhood and motherhood. Therefore, it is our aim that this book will be part of an ongoing conversation about South Asian mothering, as well as a broader discussion of mothering, culture and agency.

EFERENCES

Anderson, Kim. *Life Stages and Native Women: Memory, Teachings and Story Medicine.* Winnipeg: University of Manitoba Press. 2011. Print.

Baldwin, Sharin and Peter Griffiths. "Do Specialist Community Public Health Nurses Assess Risk Factors for Depression, Suicide, and Self-Harm Among South Asian Mothers Living in London?" *Public Health Nursing* 26.3 (2009): 277-289. Print.

Bagchi, Jasodhara. "Foreword: Motherhood Revisited." *Janani: Mothers, Daughters, Motherhood.* Ed. Rinki Bhattacharya. New Delhi: Sage Publications, 2006. 11-21. Print.

Bagchi, Jasodhara. "Representing Nationalism: Ideology of Motherhood in Colonial Bengal." *Motherhood in India: Glorification without Empowerment?* Ed. Maithreyi Krishnaraj. New Delhi: Routledge, 2010. 158-185. Print.

Bhattacharji, Sukumari. "Motherhood in Ancient India." *Motherhood in India: Glorification without Empowerment?* Ed. Maithreyi Krishnaraj. New Delhi: Routledge. 2010. 44-72. Print.

Bhattacharya, Rinki. "Preface." *Janani: Mother's, Daughter's, Motherhood.* New Delhi: Sage Publications, 2006. 22-26. Print.

Bhopal, Kalwant. "South Asian Women in East London: Motherhood and Social Support." *Women's Studies International Forum* 21.5 (1998): 485-492. Print.

Collins, Patricia Hill. "The Meaning of Motherhood in Black Culture and Mother-Daughter Relationships." *Maternal Theory: Essential Readings.* Ed. Andrea O'Reilly. Toronto, Ontario, Canada: Demeter Press, 2007. 274-289. Print.

Das Gupta, Shamita. *A Patchwork Shawl: Chronicles of South Asian Women in America.* New Brunswick, NJ: Rutgers University Press. 1998. Print.

DasGupta, Sayantani and Shamita Das Dasgupta. "Sex, Lies and Women's Lives: An Intergenerational Dialogue." *Patchwork Shawl: Chronicles of South Asian Women in America.* Ed. Shamita Das Gupta. New Brunswick, NJ: Rutgers University Press, 1998. 111-128. Print.

Daudji, Anisa, Sarah Eby, Tina Foo, Fehreen Ladak, Cameal Sinclair, Michael D. Landry, Kim Moody and Barbara E. Gibson. "Perceptions of Disability Among South Asian Immigrant Mothers of Children with Disabilities in Canada: Implications for Rehabilitation Service Delivery." *Disability and Rehabilitation* 33.6 (2011): 511-521. Print.

Green, Fiona. "Feminist Mothers: Successfully Negotiating the Tension between Motherhood as an 'Institution' and 'Experience'." *From Motherhood to Mothering: The Legacy of Adrienne Rich's of Women Born.* Ed. Andrea O'Reilly. New York: Suny Press, 2004. 125-136. Print.

Grewal, Sukhdev, Joan L. Bottorff and B. Ann Hilton. "The Influence of Family on Immigrant South Asian Women's Health." *Journal of Family Nursing* 11.3 (2005): 242-263. Print.

Gupta, Sangeeta R. *Emerging Voices. South Asian Women Redefine Self, Family and Community.* Walnut Creek: Altamira Press.1999. Print.

hooks, bell. "Revolutionary Parenting." *Maternal Theory: Essential Readings.* Ed. Andrea O'Reilly. Toronto: Demeter Press, 2007. 145-156. Print.

Kallivayalil, Diya. "Gender and Cultural Socialization in Indian Immigrant Families in the United States." *Feminism & Psychology* 14.4 (2004): 535-559. Print.

Katbamna, Savita. *"Race" and Childbirth.* Buckingham: Open University Press, 2000. Print.

Krishnaraj, Maithreyi. "Introduction." *Motherhood in India: Glorification Without Empowerment?* Ed. Maithreyi Krishnaraj. New Delhi: Sage Press, 2010a. 1-8. Print.

Krishnaraj, Maithreyi. "Motherhood, Mothers, Mothering: A Multi-Dimensional Perspective." *Motherhood in India: Glorification Without*

Empowerment? Ed. Maithreyi Krishnaraj. New Delhi: Sage Press, 2010a. 9-43. Print.

Lavell-Harvard, D. Memee and Jeannette Corbiere Lavell. "Thunder Spirits: Reclaiming the Power of Our Grandmothers." *Aboriginal Mothering, Oppression, Resistance and Rebirth*. Eds. Memee Lavell-Harvard and Jeannette Corbiere Lavell. Toronto: Demeter Press, 2006. 1-10. Print.

Maiter, Sarah and Usha George. "Understanding Context and Culture in the Parenting Approaches of Immigrant South Asian Mothers." *Affilia* 18 (2003): 411- 428. Print.

Maitra, Srabani. *Redefining "Enterprising Selves": Exploring the "Negotiation" of South Asian Immigrant Women Working as Home-Based Enclave Entrepreneurs*. Unpublished Ph.D. dissertation, Ontario Institute for Studies in Education, Toronto, 2011. Print.

Mehotra, Meeta and Toni M Calasanti. "The Family as a Site for Gendered Ethnic Identity Work Among Asian Indian Immigrants." *Journal of Family Issues* 31.6 (2010): 778-807. Print.

O'Reilly, Andrea. *Rocking the Cradle: Thoughts on Feminism, Motherhood and the Possibility of Empowered Mothering*. Toronto: Demeter Press, 2006. Print.

O'Reilly, Andrea. "Feminist Mothering." *Maternal Theory: Essential Readings*. Ed. A. O'Reilly. Toronto: Demeter Press, 2007. 792-821. Print.

Poonacha, Veena. "*Rites de Passage* of Matrescence and Social Construction of Motherhood among the Coorgs in South India." *Motherhood in India: Glorification Without Empowerment?* Ed. Maithreyi Krishnaraj. New Delhi: Sage Press, 2010. 257-291. Print

Porter, Marie. "Down Under Power? Australian Mothering Experiences in the 1950s, 1960s." *Motherhood: Power and Oppression*. Eds. Marie Porter, Patricia Short and Andrea O'Reilly. Toronto: Women's Press, 2005. 181-193. Print.

Porter, Marie. "Mothering or Motherwork?" *Theorising and Representing Maternal Realities*. Eds. Marie Porter and Julie Kelso. Newcastle, England: Cambridge Scholars Publishing, 2008. 184-200. Print.

Purkayastha, Bandana. "Interrogating Intersectionality: Contemporary Globalisation and Racialised Gendering in the Lives of Highly Educated South Asian Americans and their Children." *Journal of Intercultural Studies* 31.1 (2010): 29-47. Print.

Reed, Kate. *Worlds of Health: Exploring the Health Choices of British Asian Mothers*. Westport: Praeger. 2003. Print.

Rich, Adrienne. *Of Women Born*. New York: Norton. 1976. Print.

Silvia, Dorsía Smith. *Latina/ Chicana Mothering*. Bradford: Demeter Press, 2011.

Sinha, Rachana. *The Cultural Adjustment of Lone Mothers Living in London*. Aldershot Hans: Ashgate, 1998. Print.

Thiara, Ravi K. and Aisha K. Gill. *Violence Against Women in South Asian Communities: Issues for Policy and Practice*. London: Jessica Kingsley, 2010. Print.

Thiagarajan, M. *A Qualitative Exploration of First-Generation Asian Indian Women in Cross-Cultural Marriages*. Unpublished dissertain, Western Michigan University, 2007. Retrieved from Proquest Digital Dissertations. Web.

Reshaping, Reclaiming, Resisting

From *Parayi* to *Apni*

Mothers' Love as Resistance

RACHANA JOHRI

When a son is born we build up a web of expectations. He'll grow up, support us in our old age.... And if he turns out to be different, it is very traumatic for the parents. When a daughter is born, there is no such anxiety. She belongs to another home. I have to separate from her someday. I believe you should give her as much love as you can because ultimately she is not going to stay on with us. Then there is no expectation from her that she should earn for us. There is no give and take that is the greatest source of enmity between people. We love her, give her everything possible, educate her and generate all sorts of capabilities in her. There are no expectations from her... however she behaves. She has in- laws, she is not able to visit. We won't blame her. This is why I believe that there is no need to be upset if you have a daughter, although I too was a bit. (Johri 1999: 186)

THIS FRAGMENT from an interview with Vibha,[1] a mother of three adult daughters, captures the "essence" of the problematic issues in the mothering of daughters in north India. The narrative reveals the centrality of the ideal of marriage to the construction of womanhood and the mother-daughter relationship, particularly amongst Hindu upper class families. Drawing upon my earlier work (Johri 1999), I will focus on the narratives of three mothers whose daughters' marriages culminated in divorce. My primary argument in the paper is that despite the pressure on mothers to bear sons, evidenced in the patriarchal construction of the mothers of daughters as *banjh* (barren), a close reading of their narratives indicates the simultaneity of cultural constructions and the possibility of resistance to these. In line with Maureen Mahoney and Barbara Yngvesson (70), I argue that the politics of feminism requires an interrogation both of the oppression in women's lives and their struggles to resist these.

There have been numerous attempts to theorize resistance in the scholarship about women. My understanding of resistance is based on poststructuralist formulations which consider the embeddedness of narratives in multiple, often contradictory discourses (Weedon 112). It is the negotiation amongst different spaces that creates the possibility of resistance. As I have argued elsewhere (Johri 2007: 21), it is vital to listen to women's voices, such that neither culture nor narratives be treated as seamless wholes. While experience must be the starting point of analysis, locating resistance often requires a listening that fragments narratives into contradictory strands. A mother's narrative of love for her daughters may move between her sense of loss and powerlessness in not having borne a son, to preparing her daughter to be a good married woman. Yet the same mother may vociferously demand that her daughter be brought back home (from her in-laws' house) when she is faced with serious harm.

However, locating resisting voices requires a familiarity with the terrain within which these are articulated. In order to do so, this paper will be divided into three sections. In the first section, Contextualizing Womanhood in India, I will provide a sketch of the issues involved in being a woman in the context of urban upper class Hindu society. In the second part of the paper, Narratives of Mother Love, I will elaborate upon the construction of mother love based on narratives from my study. In the final section, Responding to Their Daughters' Distress, I will draw upon the same data to reflect upon the possibility of resistance to the dominant narrative.

CONTEXTUALIZING WOMANHOOD IN INDIA

Motherhood is one of the essentializing signifiers of womanhood and "femininity" in India (Bagchi 12). Sudhir Kakar writes, "whether her family is poor or wealthy … an Indian woman knows that motherhood confers upon her a purpose and identity that nothing else in her culture can" (1981: 56). Yet, this purpose and identity is jeopardized by the "multiple ways in which meanings have been loaded on the term 'mother' literally splitting mothers into mothers and non-mothers, pure mothers and whore mothers, mothers of sons and mothers of daughters" (Laxmi 72).

The problematic of motherhood in the Indian context is subsumed within the paradoxes in the representations and realities of women's lives in India. There is the revered figure of the mother goddess which implies a positive valuation of women as respected life-givers (Ganesh 58). At the same time, women are expected to embody female purity. Susan Wadley explains this divide through a finer analysis of cultural representations. The female in Hindu representations is both *shakti* (energy) and *prakriti* (nature). Thus woman implies a dangerous coming together of power and nature. Unbridled *shakti* is dangerous and must be brought under control. The patriarchal ideal implies that the woman uses her *shakti* to serve the interests of the male world. In control of her own sexuality the woman represents both death and fertility. With this control transferred to men she becomes benevolent and fertile. The chaste wife transfers her *shakti* to the male, making the virtue central to the preservation of male power.

Wadley points out that this dual character in the definition of femaleness shows itself in both the role prescriptions and actual roles of women in India. The dominant ego ideal for the Indian woman remains that of female purity and forbearance, in stark contrast to the powerful connotation of *shakti* (Kakar 1981: 63). This can be seen through the practice of *kanyadaan*—the unreciprocated gift of the virgin; the giving away of the bride to the husband and his family. Central to the concern with *kanyadaan* is the danger inherent in keeping a grown daughter (defined as menstruating, and therefore potentially sexual and fertile) within the natal home. *Kanyadaan* takes place as a complex set of rituals that help in the transformation of a daughter from *apni* (one's own) to *parayi* (belonging to another). While the ideal of *kanyadaan* is followed to differing extents in various communities, it forms an overarching ideology that determines womanhood amongst Hindu women (Dreze).

Once married, the primary duty of the wife is the bearing of a son to enable the performance of rituals leading to the safe passage of the *atman* (soul) after the death of the father. The ritual value of sons, and the fact that *kanyadaan* has been increasingly accompanied by dowry,[2] have resulted in a marked preference for sons in many communities in India. Practices such as passive infanticide,[3] gross neglect of a daughter after her birth and the selective aborting of the female foetus are rampant within urban and semi urban contexts. These practices are spreading to new communities, including fairly prosperous regions, (Miller; Croll 54)

In such a context, the birth of a daughter in upper class homes is often accompanied by unhappiness (Chanana 305). A wealth of data suggests that girls have less access to education and food (Palriwala 419). They also experience far greater constraints in movement. Cultural anxieties regarding the daughter's sexuality as a potential source of shame for the family and the necessity of giving her away in marriage, contrast with the power experienced by the mother of sons. These experiences of motherhood limit the possibility of the mother's love for her daughters. The mother-daughter relationship does not provide a lineage and cannot be considered to mirror the father-son relationship. Daughters may be thought of as "counterfeit children" (Das 354) a cultural difficulty in a system where the bond of mothering the daughters can be completely negated.

Despite the practice of female infanticide and the burden that is thought to be brought upon a family if they have more than one daughter, the symbolic importance of having at least one daughter is significant. First, the presence of a daughter provides the father with an opportunity to perform *kanyadaan*, which is believed to be the most virtuous of all sacrifices (Raheja and Gold 19). Daughters are also believed to represent the goddess of wealth, *Laxmi,* and the first one to be born in a family connotes good fortune. Paul Hershman reports that even while female infanticide is practiced, families desire one daughter and the one who is allowed to survive may be brought up with great indulgence. Kakar (1981: 70) suggests that the particular history of the family and the ordinal position of the daughter, along with the general acceptance towards children characterized by the Indian family, ensure for many daughters a fairly privileged position within the home. A daughter born after many sons, or one whose arrival is followed by great wealth or even the birth of another son may be greatly pampered. Barbara Miller suggests that the desire for sons does not prevent love for daughters. Mothers often pine for the bodily and psychological connection they feel with daughters even as they understand that their own significance and power within the marital family is contingent on the birth of sons (Minturn and Lambert 232).

Given the above, and because daughters are also brought up in an atmosphere of warmth, they show little rebelliousness towards the normative expectations of being women. While there seems to be greater identity exploration in urban upper class women in recent years, the majority adhere to the normative expectations of sexuality and marriage as described above. The years around puberty often become traumatic because this is the time when conscious training of the daughter to assume the role of the married woman starts. At this juncture the daughter becomes, in symbolic terms, dangerous and most women remember several reminders to the effect. Fathers and other male members of the family may withdraw attention at this juncture.

Kakar (1981: 61) believes that this is a period of enhanced warmth between the mother and the daughter since the mother is only too aware of the impending departure of the daughter and the uncertainty of her future. Indian folk songs speak of the separation as cutting a vine, and the daughter's marriage depicted like the death of the mother (Trawick 164). Sarah Lamb notes the "precious but ephemeral" quality of the mother-daughter bond as she quotes a mother from Bengal, "You just keep them with you for a few days and then give them away to another's house" (53). The theme of the daughter's departure gains significance when compared with sons who are expected to stay on and bring a wife as a daughter in-law into the family (Uberoi 114).

The experience of grief does not imply resistance to the institution of marriage. Rather, for those mothers who did not bear sons, successful mothering is signified by teaching daughters to make the transition to the status of *parayi* smoothly. Paradoxically, it is the effective severing of the relationship that indicates the capability of the mother in imparting training to the daughter. It is not surprising in such a context that the mother experiences both the longing to keep her daughter with her and anger towards a daughter who denies the necessity of marriage.

At the same time India has seen a number of changes in the position of women. Governmental policies guided more by the need for population control than the enhancement of women's reproductive choices have nevertheless had direct impact on the issue of motherhood. Family planning has introduced the idea of contraceptives and choice into the available discourses of womanhood. In the middle to upper middle classes several forces have acted together to make the birth of daughters acceptable. This has been coterminous with other transformations. The increasing entry of the middle classes into transferable jobs has meant that sons may be residing anywhere from across the oceans to the other end of the country. Daughters have become more valuable as both bread winners and sources of succor (Kakar 1997:114).

The generation of mothers that has been interviewed for this study are located within this transitional period. They experienced early marriages and early parenthood. Their daughters on the other hand have often had greater education and more freedom along with later marriage. The mothers also spent their adolescence and early adulthood in their natal homes, and were all residents of Delhi. Ten of them were upper middle class professionals. The other ten were married to men who ran their own businesses. The women in the latter group were educated but did not have professions of their own. All the women belonged to either the Punjabi community or came from the state of Uttar Pradesh and had lived most of their lives in Delhi. The participants in the study were mothers of adolescent and adult daughters and the marriage of the daughter was a primary concern for many of them. Most participants were interviewed during a phase of their lives when their daughters had either been married recently or were soon to be married. It is in the context of this transition that the possibility of mother love is analyzed in the next section.

NARRATIVES OF MOTHER LOVE

In this section I draw from the narratives of the mothers I spoke with regarding their experiences of getting their daughters married. Many mothers describe the love for their daughters as "giving her away." They describe the bond with the daughter as special, particularly because it is limited in duration. Once married or given away, their daughter can no longer be considered to be their own. Separating from her is painful but necessary. Most mothers work hard to inculcate the values that will help the daughter adjust into her new home.

The dominant narrative of the mother's love for her daughter is made up of the strands of care, compassion and loss. When mothers speak of caring for their daughters, they emphasize meeting her basic needs, giving her good food to eat and buying her clothes. It seems as if the mother knows, even if on a subconscious level, that the daughter may ultimately be deprived of tenderness and care and that as a mother, she will no longer be in a position to nurture her. Mothers and daughters share an understanding of the conditional nature of their relationship. It is inherent to loving the daughter that she must ultimately be lost.

Since daughters will be sent to another home, mothers are expected to and do train their daughters to be successful wives and daughters-in-law. While there is some preparation for a bad marriage, the dominant expectation is that the daughter be polite, well mannered and cautious. It is not uncommon for daughters to be told, "they [referring to the daughter's in-laws] are your mother and father now" (Johri 1999: 190). Mothers worry about their daughters' rebelliousness and try to inculcate the "right values" in them. A mother of four daughters, Seema anxiously tells her third daughter that she "should not take any step within the in-laws' home that brings a bad name to either family" (qtd. in Johri: 1999: 190). Seema refers to the daughter's responsibility in maintaining the honour of both her own and her in-laws' family:

> *If the marriage does not go off well, people will make nasty comments about me. If there is a fight people say, your mother has taught you nothing. That's the difference with a daughter. That's why we teach them to be respectful to everyone, love everyone, adjust yourself [sic] according to their in-laws' needs. Otherwise you will be unhappy.*

For many mothers of daughters, a sense of success is contingent upon the daughter's adaptability. This burden is not borne by the mother of sons and marks out a mother of daughters as vulnerable to social ostracism. The socialization to be polite and deferential begins at home and the mother is the chief agent in this task. Seema continues by saying,

> *If you fight with me, that's what happens to a daughter, it becomes a habit. She will fight over there [at her married home], speak loudly. Girls should speak gently, not roar like a lion. I may bear it because I am the mother but another woman will not; people will ask, what did your mother teach you?* (qtd. in Johri, 1999: 190).

A mother's task begins from the time of her daughter's birth. She must train the daughter to learn appropriate ways of communicating with a potential world of in laws.

Daughters too recognize the tying up of their identities as good wives to the status of their mother. Despite considerable unhappiness, a lovingly brought up daughter may not protest to her mother about her experiences of marriage and despite chronic anxiety, mothers maintain a distance in this regard. In this, mothers and daughters reflect "mutual understanding of oppression" (Chodorow 66). Gayatri, a homemaker and mother of two married daughters puts it poignantly:

> *Well, something happens within one's heart ... once she goes there it's her luck, it's scary at that time when you have to give away something which is your own. If she's happy in her home it's fine. Well, even kings haven't kept their daughters, not amongst Hindus.*

Another mother of three daughters, two of whom were married, agrees, "It is a terrible thing to give away your daughter but then you can't be selfish" (qtd. in Johri 1999: 191). Selfishness here refers to the comparison evoked by the image of a son who traditionally stayed on with the parents. In much of north India, sons were not expected to separate from their families. Indeed a son who had left the home evoked a sense of shame in his parents (Vatuk 73). For the son, however, this did not imply a denial of sexuality and the possibility of marriage as it would for a daughter. The cultural connotation of a son staying at home is at complete variance with that of a daughter staying on at home. Traditionally daughters stayed on only if parents were unable to arrange a marriage for them, but this was normative for a married son. A mother of daughters might wish she could ask a married daughter to stay with her just as she would have done if she had a son, but this would seem to her to be a selfish fantasy.

Given the dominant idiom of the married daughter's life as *parayi* (other) with her fate in the hands of *kismat* (destiny), mothers have traditionally experienced limited agency once a daughter is married. Although they do look forward to visits from the daughter, many mothers exercise restraint on their own initiative in this context. Mothers are expected to uncritically accept the construction of the daughter as "another" after her marriage. This acceptance by the mother also implies that unlike for the mother of a son, there is often not much to look forward to in her old age. When I asked mothers how they envisaged their old age, several of them were taken aback, almost as if they had not imagined a life after their mothering roles were over. Perhaps this was one way of negotiating the loneliness they feared once their daughters were married.

Amongst the highly educated professional women there was a greater sense of agency. The loss was also felt less, if only because of the woman's embeddedness in an alternative professional life often accompanied by independent social networks beyond those of the family. At the higher end of the continuum of education, fewer references were made about the daughter as *parayi*. Yet, the separation from the daughter through marriage was experienced as both anxiety-provoking and painful for all mothers.

RESPONDING TO THEIR DAUGHTERS' DISTRESS

Perhaps the most poignant moments during the interviews occurred as the mothers spoke of their daughters' traumas in marriage. For Vibha, Indira, and Barkha, the three mothers whose daughters' marriages culminated in divorce, the moment transformed their subjectivities as they found themselves challenging traditions to reclaim their relationships with their given-away daughters. The three women came from different contexts. Vibha did not have a professional identity. Indira worked but was not deeply involved in her profession. Barkha was a successful and dynamic artist who had traveled widely and was exposed to differing cultural contexts.

Vibha and her husband had arranged the marriage of their daughter on their own initiative. Rather keen to see their eldest daughter "settled," they seemed to have pushed their daughter who had just completed a basic college degree and had expressed a desire for further education before marriage. Vibha's narrative suggests that the daughter had been married unwittingly to a man who was sexually and psychologically abusive. In keeping with her socialization and to protect her parents from the burden of her failed marriage, the daughter did not report this to her parents. Rather, the news of their daughter's exploitation came to the family from a well-meaning acquaintance. The imposition of such a silence by a daughter on herself is not uncommon. A failed marriage is a stigma not only for a woman but also for her parents. The mother often bears the brunt of social ostracism for it has been her primary responsibility to teach her daughter "to adjust" and daughters try to protect her from this.

Vibha and her husband then engineered the escape of their daughter. Although they have eventually helped her to complete her education, take a job and marry again, the process has been a traumatizing one for the entire family. Vibha in particular has dealt simultaneously with a depressed daughter, legal battles and social ostracism. Indira was also the mother of three daughters. She was a retired teacher and described herself as fairly satisfied with her existence. At the time of our meeting, Indira was going through a harrowing phase. She had arranged marriages for two of her daughters and both had resulted in divorce. While the second daughter had coped well, the elder daughter became chronically depressed. The daughter's rejection and loss added to the mother's grief, failure and anxiety about the future. Barkha's daughter by contrast had married on her own. Having socialized her daughters for independence Barkha, despite misgivings, saw the decision as personal. Yet, she readily cared for her daughter when her daughter's marriage resulted in a divorce and is grateful that her daughter could turn to her in her time of need. From the narrative of the mother, it seems that she regrets the pain her daughter experienced but was proud that the space she had provided allowed her daughter to communicate this distress with her.

All three women whose daughters' marriages have broken have been shaped by the experience. The experience has helped them reinterpret their understanding of mothering and womanhood in significant ways. These moments have been intensely painful as Indira's narrative shows:

> *After her marriage broke, she was very depressed. One day I went out. When I returned I found she had taken out all the expensive saris from the cupboard and cut them up with a pair of scissors. Then I took her to a doctor.*

Similarly, Vibha, who had earlier insisted on her daughter's marriage, said,

> *If she is in any kind of danger, she must be brought back home by the parents. She is also a part of our body. Can we cut a finger and throw it away? She is a child made of flesh and blood, not a piece of rubbish that you will throw away and so will the in-laws. She must be educated, made to stand on her own feet. She is made of flesh and bones, not a piece of rubbish. What about her? Has she committed a crime by being born as a daughter? God sends everyone to this world, whether boy or girl. She is not our enemy that we treat her in this manner.*

The reference to the daughter as an extension of the body marks a significant departure from the ideology of the daughter as one to be given away. Vibha's assertion is a radical critique of the patriarchal world that sees the daughter as "rubbish" and a mother of daughters as a "non-mother."

The trauma was somewhat less severe for Barkha, who had expressed reservations about the ideology of *kanyadaan* through an innovative redrafting of the prayers performed at the daughter's marriage. Speaking about her relationship with her son-in-law she framed the extent and limits of the possible connection:

> When we say that you are like a son, then we mean that like she's a daughter, you are a son, that is true but this is also true that whenever there is a problem, it seems like whatever you may say, she is my daughter and he is an outsider. You know it is a matter of flesh and blood.

The loss of daughters in marriage is compensated by a son-in-law who is caring and deferential towards her parents. Mothers sometimes said that they had gained a son even though they lost a daughter. This seems to be a socially sanctioned way of endearing the son-in-law and of expressing gratitude towards him. In pointing to the difference, Barkha points to the rhetorical nature of this statement. To call a son-in-law a son is to wish that he had been one, to try and create the kind of relationship that emerges between a mother and her son. Yet it is clear in moments of conflict that the tie with the daughter has a quality of deep attachment that is lacking in the relationship with the son-in-law.

This poignant reassertion of the bodily connection seemed to be a way to negotiate with and resist the construction of the daughter as one who is given away. My argument is not however that mothers love their daughters because they have given birth to them. In insisting that daughters are bodily theirs, I suggest that the mothers are expressing a form of protest against a culture that defines them as incomplete. The repeated references to flesh and blood seem to empower them in resisting the notion of the daughter as *parayi*.

Another aspect that is apparent in Vibha's narratives is the transformation of traditional cultural symbols. Vibha recounted the militancy that characterized her fight against her daughter's in-laws' family as she compared herself to a legendary queen (*Jhansi Ki Rani*) who died fighting for her kingdom. Commenting on cultural traditions, Vibha said,

Earlier it was said that one has given away the daughter. Once that has been done you can't take anything from her. But we have to make our own mythology. We are not poor things. In fact our fate is better than that of mothers of sons. Everyone is waiting for her to die.

Vibha's sarcastic reference is to the notorious relationship between mothers-in-law and daughters-in-law in the Indian joint family. Mothers of sons wield considerable authority over the new wife of their sons, resulting in a relationship that can be bitter and hostile. Despite appearances of harmony, younger women in a household may sometimes be waiting for the older women to vacate their positions of power. In Vibha's new "mythology" the mother of daughters escapes this fate that many mothers of sons will have to someday confront.

CONCLUDING REMARKS

As I have shown through these mothers' narratives, marriage remains an essential aspect of femininity in the context of Hindu women in India. For a mother who has given birth only to daughters, love involves bearing the stigma of the "barren" woman to help daughters stand on their feet and finally to give them away in marriage. However, as I have argued earlier, the project of listening to mother love for daughters would be incomplete if it failed to hear the voice of resistance, even as it appears amidst a cacophony of other voices. My analysis in this chapter draws from the writing of feminist psychologists (Hollway 49; Weedon 167) to suggest that narratives can best be understood as multi-voiced and contradictory. The voices in a narrative reflect in part the multiple discourses that characterize society. It is in negotiating with these that resistance becomes possible.

Contemporary urban India is made up of the traditional norms of society, discourses of egalitarianism and equal opportunity as well as global images of womanhood. The mothers of daughters who participated in my research belonged to a transitional phase in India. The traditional seems to be getting reconstructed within the modern in ways that require fresh theorizing of the paradoxical aspects of gender that are emerging. Despite these changes, most mothers recognize their lower status as mothers of daughters. Mothers are also aware of problems for women, particularly within the institution of marriage. While life is better for women in some ways, most women recognize that all change is not necessarily for the better. The growing materialism of society is often referred to in terms of the grossly inhuman behaviour that women sometimes have to face within marriage. While particular marriages are considered to be oppressive, there is no critique of the institution of marriage. Despite anxiety, the institution remains idealized and one that is vital to the completion of the identity of a woman, putting the mother of daughters under tremendous pressure. There is a strong social construction of loving as giving away. However, contradictory discourses provide new spaces that mothers attempt to use. These spaces seem small in comparison to the dominance of the idiom of *kanyadaan*. Yet, mothers cannot be constructed as passive transmitters of dominant cultural ideals.

Empowering cultural representations of mother daughter relationships are rare. The strongest image involves the parting scene at the daughter's marriage. One frequent depiction shows the mother with her daughter at the time of the daughters' marriage. The mother looks on tearfully as the daughter leaves her home, the scene reinforces the ideal of the daughter who must leave home in marriage and make the transition to the status of *parayi*. This paper challenges this image. Terms such as mother, daughter, son, and woman do not occupy fixed meaning. Their meanings shift both historically and within a historical moment with the specific context within which they are used.

Listening to the voice of mothers of daughters helps to comprehend the marginality of the position they occupy. Yet it may be precisely this marginality that encourages women to search for new interpretations (Rosaldo). It is in such a context that mothers attempt within the limitations set by their personal history, as well as the availability of cultural discourses, to interpret the meaning of love for daughters. Mothers do recognize the possibility of oppression of their daughters and attempt to strengthen and protect them against it. Many of them have been able to use their positions of marginality as incomplete, insufficient women to creatively rework the idea of being mothers. In this sense it may be that they provide their daughters with greater space than is sometimes available when the daughter is embedded amongst sons. Given the cultural constraints, this resistance is only partially successful. Yet, it adds to the project of locating "the transgressions, refusals, disobedience and other forms of domination through which women resist identity"

(Sunder Rajan). Listening to the voices of mothers of daughters reveals the possibility of reversals of domination as the daughter increasingly regains the status from *parayi* to *apni.*

[1]All names are pseudonyms.
[2]Dowry refers to the practice of gifting cash and valuables to the groom and his family. The practice has spread to class and caste groups that were traditionally thought to be outside the system and is often involuntary. The increasing demand for dowry and the murder of women on the pretext that the dowry they brought was insufficient has been associated with a declining desire for daughters. While the practice has been banned, it is difficult to establish if gifts given at the time of marriage were voluntary.
[3]Miller noted that third daughters in Punjab were significantly less likely to be hospitalized, effectively allowing them to die in a form of passive infanticide. A UNFPA report indicates that the greater mortality of girls during the first two years of life can be partly accounted for by the poorer quality of medical care made available to daughters, particularly those born lower in the ordinal position. Passive infanticide was often the result of unconscious biases rather than an active decision to kill the daughter. It is likely that this has decreased after the advent of sex selection (for more information, see Guilmoto).

WORKS CITED

Bagchi, Jasodhara. "Motherhood Revisited. Foreword." *Janani. Mothers, Daughters, motherhood.* Ed. Rinki Bhattacharya. New Delhi: Sage, 2007. 11-21. Print.

Chanana, Karuna. "Female Sexuality and Education of Hindu Girls in India." *Sociology of Gender: The Challenge of Feminist Sociological Knowledge.* Ed. Sharmila Rege. New Delhi: Sage, 2003. 287–317. Print.

Chodorow, Nancy. "Family Structure and Feminine Personality." *Woman, Culture and Society.* Eds. Michelle Z. Rozaldo and L. Lamphere. Stanford: Stanford University Press, 1974. 43-66. Print.

Croll, Elizabeth. *Endangered Daughters: Discrimination and Development in Asia.* London: Routledge, 2000. Print.

Das, Veena. "*Our Work to Cry,* Your *Work* to Listen." *Mirrors of Violence: Communities, Riots and Survivors in South Asia.* Ed. Veena Das. Delhi: Oxford University Press, 1990. 345-394. Print.

Dreze, Jean. "A Surprising Exception: Himachal's Success in Promoting Female Education." *India Together* 2011. Accessed: 27 December 2011. Web.

Ganesh, Kamala. "Mother Who is not a Mother: In Search of the Great Indian Goddess." *Economic and Political Weekly* 25.42 (1990): 58-64. Print.

Guilmoto, Christophe Z. "Sex Imbalances at Birth: Current Trends, Consequences and Policy Implications." Bangkok: UNFPA Asia and the Pacific Regional Office, 2012. Web.

Hershman, Paul. *Punjabi Kinship and Marriage*. Delhi: Hindustan Publishing Corporation, 1981. Print.

Hollway, Wendy. *Subjectivity and Method in Psychology: Gender, Meaning and Science*. London: Sage, 1989. Print.

Johri, Rachana. *Cultural Conceptions of Maternal Attachment: The Case of the Girl Child*. Unpublished Ph.D. dissertation, Department of Psychology, University of Delhi. 1999. Print.

Johri, Rachana. "The Problematic Construction of Cultural Psychology from Women's Voices." *Psychological Foundations: The Journal* (2007): 13-22. Print.

Kakar, Sudhir. *The Inner World: A Psychoanalytic Study of Childhood and Society in India*. 2nd ed. New Delhi: Oxford University Press, 1981. Print.

Kakar, Sudhir. *Culture and Psyche*. New Delhi: Oxford University Press, 1997. Print.

Lamb, Sarah. *White Saris and Sweet Mangoes: Aging, Gender, and Body in North India*. Berkeley: University of California Press, 2000. Print.

Laxmi, C. S. "Mother, Mother- Community and Mother Politics in Tamil Nadu" *Economic and Political Weekly* 25.42 (1990): 72-83. Print.

Mahoney, Maureen A. and Barbara Yngvesson. "The Construction of Subjectivity and the Paradox of Resistance: Reintegrating Feminist Anthropology and Psychology." *Signs* 18.1 (Autumn 1992): 44-73. Print.

Miller, Barbra D. *The Endangered Sex*. Ithaca: Cornell University Press, 1981. Print.

Minturn, Leigh and William W. Lambert. *Mothers of Six Cultures: Antecedents of Child Rearing*. New York: John Wiley, 1964. Print.

Palriwala, Rajni. "Economics and Patriliny: Consumption and Authority Within the Household." *Women's Studies in India: A Reader*. Ed. Mary John. New Delhi: Penguin, 2008. 414-423. Print.

Raheja, Gloria G. and Ann Gold. *Listen to the Heron's Words: Reimagining Gender and Kinship in North India*. Berkeley: University of California Press, 1994. Print.

Rosaldo, Renato. *Culture and Truth: The Remaking of Social Analysis*. Boston: Beacon Press, 1989. Print.

Sunder Rajan, Rajeshwari. "Introduction: Feminism and the Politics of Resistance." *Indian Journal of Gender Studies* 7.2 (2000): 153-165. Print.

Trawick, Margaret. *Notes on Love in a Tamil Family*. Berkeley: University of California Press, 1992. Print.

Uberoi, Patricia. "Problems with Patriarchy: Conceptual Issues in Anthropology and Feminism." *Sociology of Gender: The Challenge of Feminist Sociological Knowledge*. Ed S. Rege. New Delhi: Sage, 2003. 88–126. Print.

Vatuk, Sylvia. "To Be a Burden on Others: Dependency Anxiety Among the Elderly in India." *Divine Passions. The Social Construction of Emotions in India*. Ed. O. M. Lynch. Berkeley: University of California Press. 1990. 64-88. Print.

Wadley, Susan. "Women and the Hindu Tradition." *Women in Indian Society: A Reader*. Ed. R. Ghadially. New Delhi: Sage Publications, 1988. 23-43. Print.

Weedon, Chris. *Feminist Practice and Post Structuralist Theory*. Oxford: Blackwell, 1987. Print.

Lessons of *Izzat*

MANDEEP KAUR MUCINA

THERE IS A PUNJABI WORD that I grew up hearing from a very early age in my life. This word carries more meaning than any other word I know. It is a word that forces me to think hard and fast about what I am doing, who is watching, where I am going, and how I am connected to all my relations. Every time I have spoken this word to other women like me who are Punjabi Sikh, my age, and living in Canada, we share a common understanding of what is being said and implied. This word is *izzat*. *Izzat* can loosely be translated into English as meaning honour or reputation (Badley; Lynch); however this translation does not do justice to the implications and connotations this word has for Punjabi women.[1] *Izzat* is a concept that we know and carry within us as Punjabi women, but very seldom do we speak about it inside or outside our community spaces. The stories in this paper and the discussion surrounding the concept of *izzat* are an attempt to highlight the missing voices behind discourses of *izzat* or honour based violence and the complex relationship second-generation Punjabi women have to the cultural construction of *izzat*.

This paper is divided into two parts to enable readers to ponder theoretical understandings of *izzat* as well as to gain deeper insight about how *izzat* lives in women's bodies through my personal narrative. In the first part of this paper I discuss the following points: there are dominant discourses surrounding *izzat* or honour that silence the voices of survivors of honour based violence; women, and in particular mothers, grandmothers and aunts, enforce *izzat* intergenerationally; and second generation Punjabi women are reclaiming *izzat* as a source of empowerment. In the second half of this paper I will be sharing three personal

33

narratives that challenge the dominant discourses surrounding honour and *izzat*. As a Punjabi Sikh, second-generation woman, I use my story as the basis for how I have come to understand *izzat*, as well as a way to connect to the wider story of *izzat* that lives in the Punjabi community.

DISCOURSES SURROUNDING *IZZAT*:
HEIGHTENED AND SILENCED VOICES

In the past decade the word *izzat* or "honour" has been connected to South Asian women's bodies, and their cultural knowledges or world-views, and has sprung up in various systems of knowledge production, such as the media (Armstrong; Khoday; Rogan), academia (Anwary; Gill; Kallivayalil; Niaz; Tee), as well as in policies surrounding immigration to the Western world (Werbner; Wilson). One only needs to turn a sensitive ear towards a television set and local or international newspapers to see headlines with the word "honour" embedded in stories of violence against South Asian women. For example "honour killings," "honour-related violence," "forced marriages" is repetitive "culture talk" (Jiwani) that has appeared in media excerpts that speak about violence against South Asian women in the name of honour. Yet, very seldom do we go beyond the polarized stories of honour that either portray South Asian communities as backward, tradition bound people, or defensive voices that situate honour as not representing South Asian religions.

South Asian women who are survivors of the violence that emanates from *izzat* are many times excluded from sharing their stories, as well as speaking about the cultural construction of *izzat* and its impact on their lives. This has been evident in how several high profile cases of young women who were murdered by their family in the name of honour have been publicly documented.[2] This paper is an attempt to move from this polarization and to almost humanize *izzat* and the bodies that represent these stories, through telling my story.

The act of using one's own narrative as a space for speaking about wider silencing of women has been eloquently articulated by feminists, such as Patricia Hill Collins:

> "the voice that I now seek is both individual and collective, personal and political, one reflecting the intersection of my unique biography with the larger meaning of historical times" (xii)

Collins words encourage researchers like myself to begin a conversation amongst women against this silence. A dialogue about a topic that is not only taboo for women in my community but dangerous because of its capacity to be taken up in racially charged ways by wider mainstream society, which is seen as a threat in the Punjabi community. As a second-generation Punjabi woman who has experienced the convergence of patriarchies from inside and outside my family and community, and as a survivor who has resisted the violence embedded in them, I am incited to speak out about the discourses of *izzat* that circulate in mainstream media and society, as well as in our specific South Asian communities. The silent voices in these discourses are the stories of survival and resistance that speak to the experiences of racism and oppression from dominant society and patriarchy and violence from inside.

INTERGENERATIONAL TRANSMISSION OF *IZZAT*

The first time I heard the word *izzat* was from my mother's lips. Her eyes and body held the word in such a way that I was locked and mesmerized by the message. These non-verbal cues communicated a belief, an understanding, and an identity that she not only embraced, but also subconsciously adhered to. These lessons in *izzat* were continually passed down in this non-verbal manner and eventually became a part of my very being, almost tattooed into my skin. It became a metaphoric object that was carried by the Sikh Punjabi women of my family and community, with the power to control our sexualized bodies (Grosz; Pillow). Each time my mother spoke the words *izzat* she was often referring to the "dangerous" nature of my body and how my actions had the potential to tarnish the honour of my father, family, and community. *Izzat* was something that my father owned as the patriarch of the family, yet it was in my body and in the body of the women in my family where *izzat* lived.

These lessons in *izzat* continued throughout my life and the power embedded in this discourse served many purposes. The women of my family were entrapped by the responsibility of upholding the *izzat* of generations of men in my family and community, and the men of my family were blinded by the need to regulate the actions of women in my family and community. My family can be understood as a micro example of a larger discourse that has been functioning in this very manner for many generations in most of Northern India[3] (Bose), and quite easily can be understood as an example of patriarchy that has been functioning on a global scale for generations (Bannerji).

RECLAIMING *IZZAT* AS SECOND GENERATION SOUTH ASIAN WOMEN

The role that mothers play and how women are portrayed as the ultimate teachers of *izzat* in our families and communities is a vital connection that is seldom spoken about in mainstream discourses, yet the mothers are almost always portrayed as either victims to the same culture, or perpetrators of barbaric violence (Mitchell). As I speak to my own story and experience, my mother, grandmother, and aunts were the ones who held the responsibility to pass down *izzat* to the younger generation and to do so in a way that continued the control over women's behaviours outside of the family home. This is how patriarchy continues to work globally, to encourage women to not question the control and power of these key ideologies, as well as to continue to enforce and pass them on to younger generations (Bannerji).

Yet, if we turn the gaze away for a slight moment to the history and context in which mothers play this role, we will see that the same violence, power and control is demonstrated in their lives. We see that mothers continue passing down lessons of honour or *izzat* to their daughters because of the fear that if they do not maintain these practices their daughters will be victim to violence from all the men they encounter in their lives. We see that mothers are constantly juggling a precarious balance of maintaining family and community honour, while resisting the violence embedded in the patriarchy that is demonstrated in the family, community and wider mainstream society. I recall moments where my mother would lie to my father about my whereabouts, would look the other way when she did not want to know about my outings with my friends, would defend my actions to my father when he got wind of the lies. My mother and grandmother carried the lessons of *izzat*, which involved elements of patriarchy, but they also became the ones who taught me how to resist the patriarchy and violence that had the potential to emanate from *izzat*, through their behavior and their resistance. The messengers of *izzat* are the women in our lives, but they are also the resisters and the ones to protect us when *izzat* turns ugly and violent.

Despite the patriarchal transfer from generation to generation by women of the concept of *izzat*, it may be hard to believe that there are also elements of power and resistance embedded in *izzat*. Throughout my life I have reclaimed different elements of *izzat* to embody *izzat* into my life as honour for myself rather than honour that is solely about my family and community. *Izzat* in my life is a value that reminds me of my connection to my family and community and in a sense makes me accountable to my relations. This reclaiming of *izzat* has emerged through resistance to my family, community and to wider mainstream society and is a process that I believe many second generation South Asian women are continuously going through in order to survive and resist patriarchy and cultural racism that they experience in their everyday lives.

In the following narratives, I take the opportunity to share narratives of *izzat* and the role my mother and grandmother played in passing down lessons of *izzat*. These narratives demonstrate the complex nature of *izzat* and how these knowledges are passed on. Yet these narratives are not to continue the discourses of cultural racism and the continual portrayal of South Asian communities as tradition bound and barbaric. They are meant to share a slice of my experience and how my resistance to patriarchies inside the Punjabi community and in dominant society is a vital part of *izzat* that we are not listening to. My story[4] is connected to the story of many South Asian sisters in my community, and by sharing my story I hope to ignite others to share their stories of living with *izzat* in Canada.

THE BODY OF A WOMAN

"Look what I found everyone!"

We all crowd around Perry who has found a dead snake in the middle of the road, a garter snake freshly killed by its predator, its carcass now strewn on the street, like the bones from my father's curry chicken dinner of last night.

"I think we should give it a funeral," says Preety.

Everyone agrees and Perry carefully picks up the snake with a stick and takes it to the bushes across my house. We begin digging a hole for the snake, somehow knowing that this is what you do when something dies, even though none of us has ever been to a funeral. Perry throws the snake into the hole and we cover it up.

"We should sing a song for it" says Sharon.

So we sing the only song we all know, "O Canada." Five little Punjabi children crouching around a mound of dirt, singing "O Canada" to a buried snake; of course this attracts the attention of the adults sitting inside! My mother, Perry and Kerry's mother, and Sharon and Preety's mother all stare at us from my living room window with curious eyes, wondering what we are up to. Except my mother's eyes are saying so much more. I turn to my only friends from school to figure out who my mother's eyes are piercing, trying to pinpoint what is disappointing her. Why does she have that upset look on her face? When I look closely I notice she is telling a story with those eyes and directing the moral of the story at me.

We have been having so much fun for the past hour exploring the world in my backyard. This is the first time the twins, Perry and Kerry, have come to my house with their mother. Usually I play with them at school, but today we are all together and my friend Sharon and her sister are over too. I feel so close to my friends who look and talk like me and can feel their excitement too as we sit so close to each other, almost touching one another, so innocently and genuinely enjoying this moment together. But now my mother's eyes are worrying me and I am nervous to go back to playing, so I decide to go inside for a moment. The others follow me in, either sensing my anxiousness or are bored of our playing. As soon as we go inside, Perry and Kerry's mother decides it's time to leave. Soon after, Sharon and Preety leave with their mother, and I am left in the kitchen with my mother, feeling desperately alone and worried, not knowing exactly what happened, but sensing I did something wrong.

"You have no *sharm*[5] sitting so close to Perry like that? What do you think his mother is thinking now? Who said you could play outside with boys, huh? You should be inside with me, in case I need help with anything! If you continue to do things like that you will jeopardize our *izzat*, you hear, the *izzat* of this family, your father and your own."

"But, but..." my whispering protest does not reach her ears.

Even though that moment has left me paralyzed with cold and hot flashes, my mother has moved on to other things. My head begins to feel heavy. This *izzat* that I carry for my family is starting to drag me down. I feel shame, guilt and disappointment in myself, mostly because I know how important this is and the implications of not upholding *izzat* the way my mother wants me to. I creep into the kitchen trying hard to gain my mother's respect by spontaneously washing the dishes without her harping on me to do it.

After about fifteen minutes, my grandmother sneaks up behind me and gently touches my arm with her calloused hands, a touch that always sends a glitter of warmth through my body. She tells me to move over so she can help me with the dishes. As usual she starts to complain about her knees hurting and her high blood pressure. For a moment I feel annoyed and angry at her. Doesn't she realize that I just got into trouble, and that I feel so sorry for myself right now that I don't have time to hear about her aches and pains? After a small pause my grandmother starts speaking in a rhythmic voice. I know a story is coming and I look down at the sink of dishes allowing her words to wash over me.

"Mandeep sweetheart, you need to remember that a woman's body carries a lot of responsibility. When your father was only six years old, your grandfather died very suddenly and tragically. I had three small children, your aunt was only three months old when he died and everyone was waiting for the right time to figure out what do with me. At the time I was living with my older brother, who I respect as I do God. Eventually I went to our village to the home your grandfather and I had built for our family. My brother came to me and said, "What do you want to do Khushwant, you know how this looks, with you being so young and living on your own." I knew what he was asking me. In those days widows had two choices, to get remarried to an older man, or to be watched by their maternal family, which placed a lot of burden back onto them. I knew that I did not want to be remarried, because another man would never care for my children the way that I did. So I told my brother that if he let me live on my own, I would never place myself in jeopardy of tarnishing his trust and *izzat*. I would live my life in *seva*[6] to him forever. Mandeep, do you understand what it means to live your life with your family's *izzat* in mind? To make a commitment like I did?"

I looked into my grandmother's eyes at that very moment and nodded, not totally understanding what I was saying yes to, but encouraged by her story all the same. I could feel her story burn into my soul. I felt sad for her, but also felt so proud of her for making those choices, for standing up to her brother and community. For standing up for what was important to her. But she paid a lot for those choices, something I only realized years later. My grandmother never remarried. She lived her life working hard for her children and spent a lot of energy building her reputation in the community as a respected elder. In that moment I knew that I had to claim *izzat* for myself more than for my family; and that if I respected myself and my body I was also respecting my family. But I also realized that my understanding of *izzat* was not the same as my family's. So from that day forward I vowed to never let any adult see me playing, talking, or enjoying my time with a boy. I knew that if I wanted to enjoy myself and keep my family's *izzat* in tact, I would have to be more careful.

POSSESSIONS

I am sitting in the backseat of my parents' Honda Accord with all of my personal belongings scattered around me. As I survey the small boxes, I wonder how everything that I call my own can fit into this little car. Most of *my* things include clothes, a few framed pictures from graduation, and a mound of books. Everything else that is familiar to me is at home with my family and all those things are not *mine*, but *ours*. There is a moment of clarity as I sit and stare at these *things* that I have collected over the years, *things* that have meant very little, but now in this moment mean so much to me. Is this normal? Am I normal? Is my family normal? What will *they* all think of me when I come in with such few *things*? What are *they* going to look like? Is it going to be like high school, where I have to keep my head down, keep quiet and become invisible?

My parents are driving me to the university dormitory where I will be living for the next year; driving me to a city I will be living in alone for the next four to five years. I have been planning for this moment for the past two years, to get out of our town and live on my own. So then why am I so scared? Why am I so afraid of the change that I feel coming on?

Grades 11 and 12 were the hardest years of my life so far. I knew that if I didn't do well in school I would never leave this town, my family, or my friends. Silently planning for a life where I am free from the hurtful eyes of the whiteness that surrounds me, and the protective eyes of my brown brothers that love me; secretly wishing that I wasn't this brown skinned girl, a lonely crow in a flock of robins, too big and too dark to blend in. Knowing that my only ticket out was through school, with my mind, not with this body that is disrespected by them and watched carefully by my own.

And here I am on this road to the city. To university. To a new life where nobody knows me, where I can start fresh. But how will this city be any different? Will it be any different from the taunts and ridicules of my high school peers?

There is stiff stillness in the car. My mother and father are in the front-seat, staring ahead, they have not spoken since we left the house and I can sense their sadness and worry. For the past few months I have been convincing my family that the option of moving to the city is the only way that I can pursue my education. My father was supportive of me going on to university. He was disappointed that my brother had not done well in school, like I had, so he was proud of the idea of his daughter going instead. He said he had a lot of trust in my abilities and in my commitment to him. My mother and grandmother were a little more apprehensive, they were looking at my decision with anxious eyes, anticipating what could happen if I was not regularly reminded of my *izzat*. If I forgot all the lessons of *izzat* they had taught me, what would the consequences be?

Suddenly my mother chimes into my thoughts: "*Mandeep Phuth, chata kare, theray dadi dhi Izzat theray hath may hai, kush na kari ehay Izzat krab karan tho*—Mandeep remember before you make any choice, you carry your father's *izzat* and the *izzat* of your family in your hands, don't do anything to ruin that *izzat*."

My body goes cold and hot at the same time, this moment and the words are suspended in air, they are swirling around me, like the boxes that I sit amongst in the backseat of our Honda Accord. This is the first time my mother has spoken about *izzat* to me in the presence of my father. I don't know how to respond and feel suffocated by the words that are sitting in the car, like dust blown off of an untouched bookshelf. My mother turns to look directly into my eyes, holding my gaze for what feels like years, waiting and expecting me to put those words into an invisible backpack where I am reminded of the weight and importance of what she is saying each and every time I move.

When I was living in my family home my parents had control over much of what I did from the inside. In the school space I was constrained by academics and a fairly structured environment, where I was watched by my community and a small band of brown brothers, a group of our *apna*[7] in which I grew up. In a community where my peers were a reflection of characters from American television shows about good looking, happy, middle-class, white families, I was constantly trying to find a safe place to be myself, to be human, to be visible in my skin.

41

However, my parents knew as much as I did that from this day forward I would be venturing into spaces that *I* had more control over, spaces that they could not visualize or understand because of the limits of their accessibility to those spaces. I was entering a space that was unique to my upbringing in Canada, they could only imagine what my everyday encounters would entail and many times their imagination was wilder than reality. I was entering into the world of individuality with their *izzat* in my hands, a risk they undertook with uneasiness, yet they trusted me to know what it all meant.

I saw the words of my mother in front of me, shrouded in responsibility and expectations. I was afraid of those words, but felt a mixed sense of importance as well. Eventually, I took the words of *izzat* imparted on me that pivotal first day, carefully placed them in my invisible backpack and carried this with strength and pride into the university dormitory.

HEADLINES

"And then Chacha Ji said, 'What, he only stabbed her eleven times? I would have stabbed her 17 times just to make sure the job was done right.' Then Amar said, 'Why not 27 times?' ...I was so shocked and scared when I heard them joking around like that.... Are you sure you want to go through with this Mandeep?"

My sister is giving me a play-by-play of a conversation my family was having around the TV when the murder of Amandeep Atwal hit the news. This is the first I was hearing of this conversation. Since I stopped living with my family after moving away for university, my sister was my lifeline to the daily conversations that happened in my family home.

"DAUGHTER STABBED FOR RUNNING AWAY WITH BOYFRIEND."
"HONOUR KILLING HIDES RACIST MOTIVES."
"B.C. MAN KILLS DAUGHTER IN A FIT OF RAGE AFTER HEARING ABOUT WHITE BOYFRIEND."

The headlines were everywhere I looked, and we all knew the story well. Amandeep did what we all do; she dated in secrecy. However she went on to do something even more brave: that is, tell her family about her secret, which subsequently led to her death at the hands of her father. This story brought up past stories of suicide, murder, domestic violence of young women in our community—the Punjabi community. Jassi Sidhu[8] was remembered in that moment, not in a "never again" manner, but in a "damn, not again" way. This time Amandeep's story was reaching a little too close to home for me.

"Mandeep, are you going to tell Dad about David?" My sister looks at me with worried eyes, almost begging me not to take the same route that Amandeep took.

David—the love of my life, my soul mate, best friend and secret lover, yes, secret. We had been dating each other for the past year since I finished my Bachelor's degree and I was not ready to bring him home to my father. You see, David is far from being Sikh, Punjabi, or even Indian: he is Black.

I want to hear the details of the conversation again to make sure I heard correctly what my sister was telling me, but am too afraid to ask, knowing that most likely there is no mistake in what I heard. My brother and my uncle were joking about Amandeep's death. Behind those jokes, even my little sister could detect their allegiance with Amandeep's father, who was upholding his *izzat*. She was just as scared as I was, of what the men in our lives were capable of, what they felt responsible for.

"Was Dad there, Sonia?"

"Yeah, but he didn't say anything"

Of course he didn't. My father doesn't speak, unless he really feels the need to. I start breaking into a sweat, imagining the moment that I tell him about David. Will he go into a "fit of rage" like Amandeep's father? Will he do anything to protect his *izzat*? Our family *izzat*?

I think about *izzat* and the subtle ways my mother and grandmother have taught me to carry the *izzat* of my family and community, but to carry my own *izzat*, which is what I have worked on over the years. I think about my relationship to *izzat* and how it has changed from this piece of myself that I hid from everyone I knew, to something I carry, less for my family and more for myself. It has transformed into a part of me that I recognize and embrace. Now I am afraid that this will be taken away from me once I tell my father about David. By sharing with my father this secret, I am sharing all the secrets I have been keeping: alcohol, partying with my friends, going on trips where there are boys. Lies and secrets.

I have kept this part of my life a secret because I don't think my parents will understand. I think they might see it as shameful behavior, even though I think it is not. I do these things because I like to, and because am expected to by my friends: friends who don't come from this life, this house, this skin. So the only way I can do what I want while remaining my father's daughter is to keep that part of my identity a secret.

My friends don't know much about my family life either. They often ask me why I go to visit my family almost every other weekend, why I talk to my parents almost every day, why I lie to my parents about what I am doing and where I am going. My friends just don't understand how I understand my family and why they want to keep me in this gilded cage, why they are invested in my behavior more than other parents... white parents. They don't understand how as much as my family's desire to be a part of every decision in my life can be annoying, it is how I am connected to them. It is about the respect and love I have for them.

This gilded cage that many *apna* girls I know sit in is such a beautiful cage from the inside, but from the outside it may appear cold and constraining. It may look cruel. Yet, this is the part that they don't understand. I do have a key to my gilded cage, as did Amandeep. We use that key when we need to, and at other times we choose not to. It is when that key is taken away from us and we are expected to choose the cage or the world outside of the cage that the polarity of our identities become real. Is this really a choice? Inside it is comforting, beautiful, loving, yet constraining, and confined. Outside there is autonomy and experiences I have not seen or felt, yet there is the everyday experience of being an outsider, or being judged by those who think I am different, exotic, too ethnic. Those who tell me I smell of "curry" and "India," yet have they ever been to India? Do they even know what curry is? They tell me that my parents are cruel and backwards, but what part of their intervention makes them cruel? They may not know what leads my parents to be this way, but I do. I know the fear they have of change, of seeing their children in an entirely different space and context from where they grew up. Choices seem like privileges, but is there any choice when both sides are restricting?

So where was the choice for Amandeep? Where was the choice for Jassi? Where is my choice?

"Mandeep? Mandeep? MANDEEP... are you going to tell Dad?" my sister chimes in with that dreaded question again. This time I can't avoid it, I have to answer her, I have to answer David, and I have to answer myself.

"Yes, Sonia, I have to...."

ENDNOTES

[1]For this paper, I situate my experiences of *izzat* within the Punjabi Sikh community in Canada.

[2]I am referring here to the case of Jaswinder Kaur Sidhu, Aqsa Parvez, the three sisters Zainab Shafia, Sahar Shafia, Geeti Shafia and Rona Mohammed.

[3]I am focusing only on Northern India geographically. As well the focus is on the Punjabi community of India for this paper. This is due to the fact that India, the culture, its people, and its knowledges are quite diverse and historically each region has its own history and knowledges that are specific to the people of that area. It would be impossible to gather and portray the history of all the people of India, and to homogenize a complex concept like *izzat* to the entire nation and its heterogenous people. By focusing specifically to a community that has existed in Northern regions of India for centuries, I will be able to focus on the concept of *izzat* and contribute to not further essentializing the entire South Asian community and their understandings of *izzat*.

[4]All names have been changed to pseudonyms in the three narratives, except for my own, since I have self identified as the subject of the story.

[5]Shame.

[6]Self-less service.

[7]People of our own community, Punjabi Sikhs.

[8]Jassi Sidhu was a Punjabi-Canadian girl who grew up in British Columbia and was allegedly murdered in India through a plan orchestrated by her mother and her uncle in Canada. It is suspected that she was murdered because she had ruined the family's honour by marrying a poor, lower caste man who she had met in her family's village in Punjab, India. She married him despite vehement opposition from her parents. She was killed while in India visiting her husband.

WORKS CITED

Anwary, Afroza. "Teaching About South Asian Women Through Film." *Teaching Sociology* 31.4 (October 2003): 428-440. Print.

Armstrong, Jane. "Death of a secret lover: B.C. jury hears tragic tale of a defiant daughter who hid affair." *The Globe and Mail* March 3, 2005. Accessed July 1, 2009. Web.

Badley, Brenton. H. *The Popular Dictionary: English and Roman Urdu,*

Roman Urdu and English. Rev. ed. Lahore: Brothers Publisher, 1993.

Bannerji, Himani. *Inventing Subjects: Studies in Hegemony, Patriarchy and Colonialism*. New Delhi, India: Tulika Books, 2001. Print.

Bose, Mandakranta, ed. *Faces of the Feminine in Ancient, Medieval, and Modern India*. New York: Oxford University Press, 2000. Print.

Collins, Patricia Hill. *Black Feminist Thought: Knowledge, Consciousness, and the Politics of Empowerment Perspectives on Gender. Volume 2*. New York: Routledge, 1991. Print.

Gill, Aisha. "Governing Violence: Gender, Community and State Interventions." *Community Safety Journal* 4.2 (April 2005): 37-45. Print.

Grosz, Elizabeth. *Space, Time, and Perversion*. London: Routledge, 1995.

Jiwani, Yasmin. *Discourses of Denial: Mediations of Race, Gender, and Violence*. Vancouver: University of British Columbia Press, 2006. Print.

Kallivayalil, Diya. "Gender and Cultural Socialization in Indian Immigrant Families in the United States." *Feminism and Psychology* 14.4 (2004): 535-559. Print.

Khoday, Amar. "'Honour killings' hide racist motives." *The Toronto Star* March 8, 2005. Accessed July 1, 2009. Web.

Lynch, Owen. *Divine Passions: The Social Construction of Emotion in India*. Berkeley: University of California Press, 1990. Print.

Mitchell, Bob. "Father and son plead guilty to murdering Aqsa Parvez." *The Toronto Star* June 15, 2010. Accessed November 15, 2012. Web.

Niaz, U. "Violence Against Women in South Asian Countries." *Archives of Women's Mental Health* 6 (2003): 173-184. Print.

Pillow, Wanda. "Exposed Methodology: The Body as a Deconstructive Practice." *Working Ruins: Feminist Poststructural Theory and Methods in Education*. Ed. E. St. Pierre and W. Pillow. New York: Routledge, 2000. 199-220. Print.

Rogan, Mary. "Girl Interrupted: The Brief Life of Aqsa Parvez." *Toronto Life* (December 2008): 53-58. Print.

Tee, Karen A. *Between Two Cultures: Exploring the Voices of First- and Second-Generation South Asian Women*. Ph.D. Dissertation, University of British Columbia, Canada, 1997. Print.

Werbner, Pnina. "Veiled Interventions in Pure Space Honour, Shame and Embodied Struggles among Muslims in Britain and France." *Theory, Culture and Society* 24.2 (2007): 161-186. Print.

Wilson, Amrit. "The Forced Marriage Debate and the British State." *Institute of Race Relations* 49.1 (2007): 25-38. Print.

Children's Identity Formation in the Sikh Diaspora

An Exploration of Sikh Mothers' Roles

TARNJIT KAUR

FEMINIST MOTHERING within faith-based communities is a relatively unexplored area of the mothering discourse. As diverse, multicultural societies and liberal-secular democracies across the globe grapple with navigating the politics of identity and fulfilling their responsibilities of protecting the rights of all individuals and groups, particular groups continue to be marginalized. Public displays of *personal* religiosity expressed through *visible* religious identities have become highly racialized. In such fraught environments the role of the mother in both protecting and navigating her children's religious identity and socialization is itself highly political work. In this paper I will show the active role Sikh mothers play in cultivating a *visible* Sikh identity for their children through maintaining the interconnectedness of Sikh ethics and Sikh practices in their children's religious socialization.

Visible Sikh identity is most conspicuously imprinted on the *male* Sikh body by the presence of the *kesh*[1] (long unshorn hair) usually covered by a *dastaar*.[2] The *kesh* together with the *dastaar*, with the intended symbolism of a crown, became mandatory attire for the followers of the Sikh faith at a point in history when Sikhs were severely marginalized. It was an expression of sovereignty, in the face of persecution, when only elites were permitted to wear such head coverings. The Sikhs' *kesh* is their "Star of David," their "cross," their "hijab." It is also an outward identifier signifying them as the "other" who is not adhering to normative behavior and is clearly refusing to assimilate into wider mainstream (hegemonic) culture.

The impetus for this chapter arose from the conflict I experienced as a Sikh feminist mother of a male child, living in the North American Sikh diaspora. I was torn by maternal desires to shield my son from racism, bullying and *othering*, and a sense of responsibility to defend my child's right to a religious identity. An identity that he was born into, but was too young to proactively choose for himself. I sought answers to questions such as: Why is the onus only on mothers to be the preservers and transmitters of religious identity? Why does Sikh identity continue to be imprinted most visibly on the *male* Sikh body through the conspicuous presence of the turbaned *kesh*? Following the Sikh practice of dealing with such quandaries through requesting advice from the Sikh *sangat*[3] I chose to interview Sikh mothers and Sikh men about their experiences with cultivating and preserving a visible Sikh identity.

Through this chapter I hope to initiate dialogue on the questions I posed above, and capture how Sikh mothers, through cultivating a Sikh religious identity for their children, express a form of empowered mothering. I will begin this paper with a short introduction to *Sikhi*, followed by the methodology, the main themes that emerged from my interviews, and a discussion about the implications of this work.

INTRODUCING SIKHI

Sikhi—the Sikh way of life and the Sikh faith—emerged in the lifetime of its founder, Guru Nanak (born 1469 in South Asia), followed by a succession of nine human Gurus.[4] The authority of the Guru was then bestowed on the Sikh scripture, a collection of poetical compositions, the *Guru Granth Sahib*. The *Guru Granth Sahib* is primarily an exaltation of the Divine and gives intimations of how spiritual enlightenment can be attained through union with the Divine (*Nabha*) by "remembering" the Divine (*simran*) and offering selfless service (*seva*) to society. The concept of *seva* within *Sikhi* is embedded within the context of social and political action concisely described by the three inseparable directives: *nam japo, kirat karo* and *vand shako. Nam japo* (literally 'recitation of the divine name') refers to the individual's practice of meditation (*simran*); *kirat karo* (earning an honest living) is the practice of truthfulness in all dealings, which benefits the individual, family and society at large; and *vand shako* corresponds to the sharing of a percentage of one's earnings with others, especially those in need.

Sikh religious and cultural identity first became apparent with the establishment of the first Sikh community at Katarpur on the banks of the River Ravi in Punjab by Guru Nanak in the early 1500s (Singh, P.). The community incorporated the institutions of *Sikhi,* such as the open kitchen (*langar*), sitting and eating together without class, caste or gender distinctions (*pangat*), and the gathering in solidarity and community (*sangat*), all of which are an integral part of *Sikhi* and demonstrate a commitment to social and economic justice (Singh, P.). The community also confronted patriarchy and strictly prohibited forms of subjugation directed towards women at that time, such as not allowing widows to remarry, dowry, female infanticide, veiling of women and *sati.*[5] By the sixteenth century education for women was made mandatory in the Sikh community and women were appointed to public leadership roles.

As the Sikh community evolved, the requirement of five markers of Sikh faith was concretized by the formation of the *Khalsa*[6] by Guru Gobind Singh (the tenth Guru). These five markers of faith for both women and men, the most conspicuous of which is the *kesh,* serve as a unifying collective identity and a visible commitment to the Sikh faith.

METHODOLOGY

The narratives presented here are derived from in-person, telephone and email-based interviews. Interviews of twelve Sikh mothers (two single mothers and ten women living as part of a nuclear family) and five Sikh men, all of varied backgrounds in terms of their level of education, level of adherence to *Sikhi* and migration history (currently resident in Britain, the United States and Canada) were conducted following a snowball sampling method. The Sikh women were asked a series of open-ended questions concerning their role in their children's upbringing. Adult Sikh men were approached to specifically recount their childhood experiences of maintaining *kesh*. I conducted interviews through email and telephone conversations. To maintain the anonymity of the interviewees I have used the name "Kaur" for Sikh women and "Singh" for Sikh men followed by numerals to identify the different contributions.[7]

The interviews were transcribed and commonalities were drawn using an inductive approach (Attride-Stirling; Braun and Clarke). The method adopted for data collection in this work has limitations. The Sikh women and men, by their very agreeing to be interviewed, cannot be regarded as a random sample of members of the Sikh community. By willing to be interviewed they have already demonstrated that they are a specific section of the larger Sikh community, which values *Sikhi* research and education and therefore has more of a vested interest in the topics that were discussed. As well, most of the interviewees grew up in the diaspora, and had been subjected to discrimination growing up themselves, as Sikhs. Therefore they were more conscious of how racism and gender biases might affect their children. The two interviewees who grew up in India were able to speak to prejudices experienced by Sikhs in India. In this way, this group of participants was able to articulate their experiences as Sikhs in a way that not everybody can. As such, they do not represent the whole Sikh community, but rather a sub-community within it.

BEING A MOTHER, BEING A SIKH MOTHER: THE LIVED REALITY

There were four main themes that emerged in the mothering practices of the Sikh women who were interviewed, that cut across their diversity in terms of upbringing, level of education and religiosity. These same themes also emerged when discussing their own upbringing and how it influenced their subsequent understanding of *Sikhi*. The main themes from the interviews with the Sikh men also fell within these same parameters. These themes are as follows: (1) Modeling and mentoring, (2) Giving voice and building community (3) Social justice, and (4) Being accepted.

Modeling and Mentoring

All the Sikh mothers interviewed considered their own behavior to be important; they did not necessarily censure themselves. Instead they took care to be consistent and to "model" behavior that would enrich the spiritual lives of their children. Kaur3 said "becoming a mother inspired me to live a religious life focused on the divine and to instill family values and spirituality into my children and grandchildren."

Five women (Kaur1-3, 6, 7) embarked on a daily routine of increased meditation (*simran*) and prayer during pregnancy. They and others (Kaur5, 10) sought to foster a spiritual practice into their day, especially first thing in the morning and as part of their children's bedtime routine. Children would often engage in such practices by mimicking their mothers' behavior without being instructed to.

Kaur2, 6, 11, 12 and Singh 3, 4 mentioned that their earliest memories of *Sikhi* were of their own mothers practice of *simran* and prayer. Kaur6 said that growing up "we practiced the tenets of *Sikhi* in our household

... doing the right thing, *seva, naam simran*" and in her role as a mother to her daughter "[i]t is my hope, as her guide, and her *sevay-daar,*[8] her parent, her teacher, to provide an inspirational, spiritual space that is informed by *Sikhi* but never forced upon her."

Kaur1, 5, 9 and 12 also expressed that the modeled behavior should extend to their own outward manifestations of identity. Kaur9 and Kaur12 decided to start maintaining their own *kesh* after having not done so for most of their adult lives. Kaur9 said "how can I cut [my] hair but then [my child(ren)] be expected to keep theirs?" Kaur1 started to keep her own hair covered at all times. The importance with which the physical aspects of identity are held is apparent by Kaur5's statement:

> The life-changing episode of my life, of being widowed, means that the keshdhari[9] image of my husband isn't here anymore. This means that I have the ultimate responsibility of bringing up my children as Sikh in Britain.

However, the role that modeled behavior plays is highly complex; it is interesting to note that although Singh3, 4 and 1 all grew up with fathers who maintained shorn hair, they themselves, either of their own volition (Singh3 and 1) or under the instruction of their mother (Singh4), each maintained *kesh* in their adulthood. These Sikh men demonstrated a significant level of commitment to Sikh identity in their early teens (Singh1 and Singh4) or as adults (Singh3). Through a process of self-education, independently of their parents, where they relied on the *Gurudwara*[10] or Sikh student societies at college or university as sources of inspiration as well as information, they came to solidify their identities.

Giving Voice and Building Community

Sikh mothers strive to provide an outlet for expression for their children, as well as build a community that validates their children's Sikh identity. Kaurs1-9, 12 spoke about how they taught their children *kirtan*[11] and meditation to nurture the spiritual dimension to their children's development. Kaur6 describes why she teaches *kirtan* to her daughter,

> to provide a strong, spiritual space for her to develop her own spirituality just like her cognitive or physical development. Sikhi will be a space that helps develop her emotional intelligence as

well—those values and ethics espoused by the Sikh stories will
encourage the development of emotional intelligence.

Kaur4 shares similar thoughts, she states, "a sense of spirituality can teach our children so much about the world such as compassion and respect for others."

The process of learning *kirtan* is an arduous one, but for the mothers, its importance far outweighed the difficulties of teaching *kirtan* to their children. Kaur5 said, "Learning (and performing) *kirtan* is a serious investment of mine and my children's time and energy." The benefits of this investment are reiterated by Singh4, "[My mum] pushed us a lot [to learn to do *kirtan*], there were difficulties, we rebelled, but I am so glad that she pushed us since I am very happy now being able to do and teach *kirtan* now." It has become central to Singh4's spiritual life; "*kirtan* is an outlet, it is a way of expressing myself, *kirtan* peaces me out, calms me down, keeps me connected." Singh2 said that *Sikhi* shaped him,

> …in some really powerful ways. One was being exposed to kirtan
> and learning kirtan at a young age—that was the first music I
> ever played and where I initially found my singing voice I think.
> And the beauty of it was always very apparent to me I think.

With the desire to instill a sense of spiritual intelligence which requires being tuned into the child's emotional development, there is a concomitant culture among the Sikh mothers interviewed, of varying degrees of attachment mothering that is sensitive to the child's emotions. In many families this style of mothering is just a continuation of practices carried out in previous generations (Kaur2, 4, 6). In others it is very much a mothering style that was adopted after self-education (Kaur 12). Some mothers spoke explicitly of cultivating a sense of spirituality through sensitive mothering (Kaur2, 4, 6,7) where the basis of the connection with the Divine is embedded in the mother-child bond.

Mothers also developed strategies to develop a community that would support the nurturing of *Sikhi* for their children. Kaur9 said, "The support and resources are built into our lives as they are, without any effort on our part," referring to how her children's grandparents were the main sources of knowledge and the practice of *Sikhi*, requiring little or no input from her. Others such as Kaur1, who regularly "takes her daughter to the *Gurudwara* ... to be around our *Gursikh*[12] friends and their children," and Kaur4 recognize that active participation in community building activities such as partaking in the *langar* and *sangat*, contribute to their children's sense of belonging and involvement. Kaur8 talked of how the *Gurudwara* plays a role beyond religious instruction, "I have sent him to *Gurmat* camp.[13] ...I deliberately made the decision when he wanted to join a soccer club that he did it through the *Gurudwara*, I proactively try to maintain the connection with the *Gurudwara*."

The rewards of the efforts put in by the mothers both on their own as well as through the community they have cultivated around them, are expressed in the quote by Kaur4 who states that for her son, "[t]he religious and spiritual identity has actually become the calming point, the place where I think he will find that sense of belonging and community despite many challenges."

Social Justice

Kaur12 was initially attracted to *Sikhi* because of its social justice message. She said, "*Sikhi* exemplifies all the ideas that I hold dear, ideas of social justice, a commitment to equality, fighting all forms of oppression." Singh2 stated that he became "an activist and organizer and [being] a radical stems from experiencing so much racism and bigotry growing up." He explains further,

> *Once I found my voice to engage in dialogue about the injustice of this reality and I was supported and empowered around it, my life began to change in a major way. Soon I began to see the connection between what I experienced and all the other various forms of oppression and how they're rooted in the same thing. Keeping my* kesh *and wearing my turban became a part of my resistance to assimilation and racism.*

Kaur4 echoes his sentiments when she reflects upon what it would mean to be a successful mother.

> *Success would look like raising a son who is happy in his own skin, compassionate about others and willing to stand up for basic human rights that affect all global citizens.... His Sikh*

*identity will be reflected in his daily actions rather than any
outward show.*

However, a disconnect between this message of social justice in the
theory and practice of *Sikhi*, is most apparent in the prevalence of son
preference. The desire for male off-spring manifests itself in many forms:
preferential treatment of boys in terms of food, education and general
attention and aborting a female fetus specifically because of its sex.

Kaur1 and 2 experienced significant negativity from their mother-
in-laws since they had had only daughters, despite the whole extended
family being *Amritdhari*[14] Sikhs. Kaur2 explains,

> *With Sikhi's egalitarian philosophies, it is challenging to hear
> Sikhs express their disappointment with the arrival of our blessed
> girl child. Women are not positioned as "less-than" in the phi-
> losophy of this young religion, but rather, we are all meant to be
> equal. Both my partner and I become disheartened when we hear
> the problematic anti-women/anti-girl-child rhetoric. We expect
> better from Sikhs—especially in this generation. I have always
> believed that Sikhi is very feminist and [I am] thankful I have a
> spiritual space that is rooted in feminism—it is unfortunate that
> not everyone gets that!*

For other mothers, insidious forms of control were exerted over them
by their in-laws in other forms—such as whether or not they adopted
the outward markers of Sikhism. Kaur8 said, "My in-laws degraded
me because I did not follow the outward behavior (of *Sikhi*); they were
abusive, they lied and cheated. They did not follow the core values of
Sikhi." In a similar vein, women who do choose to adopt the outward
markers of *Sikhi* were also criticized by in-laws. When Kaur1 decided
to don a *keshki*[15] of her own volition, she faced opposition from her
Amritdhari mother-in-law who preferred her to dress in an excessively
lavish fashion typical of Indian brides.

Kaur7 feared that her own experiences of being subjected to pressures
to conform would be repeated and she felt compelled to protect her
daughter from any such onslaughts. Through a process of continued
negotiation she created a safe space for her daughter to explore her own
identity in her own time,

I do not want anyone telling my daughter what she should do, how she should keep her hair and cover her hair.... Sikhi is not merely defined in terms of keeping the outward identity, it is not just about hair. I do not want my child to be identified in such terms.

However, some of the Sikh mothers (Kaurs1, 2, 5, 8, 10, 12) explicitly recognized that these controlling and conforming measures directed towards them as women, had more to do with the structures of patriarchy than with *Sikhi*.

BEING ACCEPTED

Sikh children often suffer alienation because of racism, especially in environments where they are a minority. The Sikh Mothers I interviewed played an active role in mediating that alienation. All of the interviewees were very cognizant of their own and their children's desires to "fit in" and to feel accepted both by the Sikh and the wider community they live in. Of the 12 Sikh mothers interviewed in this work nine are committed to maintaining their children's *kesh*. They knew that in doing so, their child would be marked as different, and they had to make a conscious effort to alleviate the stress this may cause for their children.

Singh2 describes what it was like growing up as one of two Sikh boys in his small town (the other being his brother). Unlike the mothers in this study, his parents were not fully aware of the racism he faced and therefore were not able to provide him with the supports he needed. Singh2 explicitly describes this experience,

[My]sense of isolation was very acute and very intense growing up. I won't lie, it was really, really hard and really painful. I was not a confident child at all and didn't know how to process all the shit I was going through at school. I didn't talk with my parents or brother about it at all. I have no idea how my life would have been different if I felt like there was a space to talk about this stuff with my family. But if I ever raise Sikh kids with their kesh, I will certainly be as proactive as possible to discuss all these issues around harassment and bullying, self-confidence and anger.

Positive affirmation of Sikh identity in the diaspora is an ongoing issue that also concerns Sikh Mothers. Kaur6 states,

> *I honor the commitment that Amritdhari Sikhs have made and how every day, every minute, their outward identity, positions them as Sikhs. And in today's climate, this religious commitment is often misinterpreted as being zealots or fanatics. The turban is a spiritual marker, a religious marker but has also become a part of the "terrorism" social discourse. And it takes a great deal of commitment to adhere to this outward projection of your religious/spiritual identity. I have the utmost respect for people who engage in that every day.*

Kaur11 and Kaur7, both recent immigrants to Canada, expressed how this discrimination against turbaned Sikh men was also evident in India. For them, the very process of migration caused them to re-examine their value system and how it relates to their personal and collective identities. Kaur7 also became more conscious of the racial and religious inequities in India:

> *Just as the white, middle-class male is the idealized image in Canada, so is the clean-shaven, fair-skinned man in India. Just as the white, middle-class male is in positions of power in Canada, so in India all positions of power and prestige are occupied by clean-shaven men.*

Due to their recognition of the discrimination their children may experience, the Sikh mothers I interviewed, sought to take a proactive approach to strengthening their children's identities. For example they were ready and prepared to deal with any sort of bullying if it occurred in the school environment. Kaur10 gave presentations on *Sikhi* at her children's schools and Kaur1 said, "If someone did make fun of her or teased her at school, I [would] go into the school and give a talk about *Sikhi*. I think once people are informed and educated about *Sikhi* then there will not be any bullying."

Mothers had a greater awareness of the issues their children may be facing, as well as a greater understanding that their children were growing up in a multicultural society in which their *Sikhi* was just one aspect of their identity that needed to be supported in order for them to feel accepted. They are careful to build relationships with people from all cultures. As Kaur8 shows,

> *I do worry about my imprint on my son in terms of his identity, I am not teaching him just about religion, I actively teach him about culture in general. He has kept his kesh from one year old (he is now six years old) and has been surrounded by children of all backgrounds.*

Kaur9 and her husband also took a bicultural approach to bringing up their child[ren]: "We are raising our child[ren] the way we are, we are Indian but we are also proud to be Canadian too. We are still struggling with it sometimes." In contrast Singh3 felt that *Sikhi* and being Canadian are completely compatible. He said, "I am a Sikh who is British Columbian Canadian."

DISCUSSION AND CONCLUSIONS

In recent years within the mothering discourse, feminist mothering theorists have defined *empowered* mothering as "a mode of mothering that affords and affirms maternal agency, authority, autonomy and authenticity and which confers and confirms power to and for mothers" (O'Reilly 15). In the following I shall seek to derive these characteristics of *empowered* Sikh mothering distilled from the thematic analysis in this chapter, as well as extend the definition of empowered mothering to also include advocacy.

The narratives presented in this work strongly indicate that the practice of *Sikhi* often occurs in a predominantly Punjabi cultural context where there is a prevalence of patriarchy. Despite this, women are choosing to align themselves with *Sikhi* and in doing so express their agency. Whilst not denying the pervasiveness of patriarchal family dynamics, gendered violence and son preference, gender based inequalities are continually being challenged and eroded by the efforts of Sikh women themselves.

In the diaspora, Sikh women are increasingly present in the public spheres of professional life (Bhachu; Brah). In the private sphere of the home, Sikh women continue to negotiate and challenge the impositions of patriarchy. This was demonstrated in the narratives above when women's dress-code was being regulated and especially when there was interference in their mothering role. The implications of this continuous resistance to patriarchy is that the boundaries for establishing maternal and parental authority in child-rearing and in matters concerning religious socialization often need to be established and negotiated with members of the extended family as well as the wider communities.

Maternal authority is apparent in how mothering and motherhood is situated within *Sikhi* through the representations of the mother within the Sikh scripture. The recurrent mentions of the mother-child dyad in Sikh scripture are indicative of her importance. It is a poetical device, a metaphor employed repeatedly, for describing the reciprocal bond between the creator and the created (*Guru Granth Sahib* 105, *Guru Granth Sahib* 164). In such references, idealized expressions of motherhood through the more stereotypical images of mothering, as being the nurturer and the provider of sustenance are reiterated. It is, however, in the explicit mention of the bodily functions, the innate biological processes of the female body, that the Sikh scripture subvert the prevalent religious and cultural hegemonies (Singh 1993). The mention of menstruation within the *Guru Granth Sahib* (*Guru Granth Sahib* 140, *Guru Granth Sahib* 473) as a life-giving process and a life-affirming power, rather than in the hushed tones of a taboo subject or as a source of pollution, further asserts the authority of the mother. Likewise lactation is explicitly depicted in *Gurbani*[16] to indicate the close attachment of the child to the mother as a celebrated unique bond and is employed as a metaphorical device synonymous with achieving spiritual salvation through the union with the Divine.

In their mothering styles Sikh women were often enacting aspects of Sikh scripture—modeling and mentoring, giving voice, building community, and social justice, are all central themes within Sikh thought. These patterns of behavior, intimately connected to Sikh practices, have not been prescriptively laid out anywhere. Rather, through a combination of learnt behavior and informed choices, the Sikh mothers exert their maternal autonomy in deciding upon their mothering styles.

All the mothers interviewed expressed that their primary maternal intention is to equip their children with good values and ethics and the tools required to leading meaningful lives. *Sikhi* is seen as the framework and toolkit for achieving these objectives. In doing so, these mothers demonstrate maternal authenticity. They do not merely follow ritual or religiosity in a dogmatic fashion but rather through critical assessment choose *Sikhi* as the basis of their children's upbringing.

Repeatedly throughout the narratives Sikh women talked of the relevance of *Sikhi* to their lives in the diaspora. It is also clear that experiences such as "[t]he hearing or reciting of *bani*[17]—being stirred by its rhythms—is shared by the *sangats* of the past and the present (and, perhaps also the future)" (Singh, N. 1993: 47) constitute the larger narrative of the Sikh community. Through the active participation in Sikh community life, especially centered around the *Gurudwara*, a sense of collective identity is being formed. As a part of this, the outward markers have importance and the majority of the mothers (nine of the twelve mothers) interviewed are committed to keeping their children's *kesh*.

The highly racialized Sikh identity in the diaspora, where the imbrications of identities of race, religion, class and gender intersect, is marginalized on multiple levels. Growing up in predominantly Anglo-Saxon environments such as North America or Britain, young people suffer alienation from their peers (Aulakh), bullying (Sikh Coalition), and racial discrimination in schools (Verma), workplaces and other social spaces. There have been numerous instances, from anecdotal stories, that due to this alienation young people grow up lacking self-confidence, self-pride and/ or experience a sense of disorientation. There is a sense that these young people fail in self-efficacy and enter adulthood without consolidating a strong sense of identity (Klassen and Georgiou). In the post-9/11 world the turban (and therefore *kesh*) is seen to embody the enemy and the terrorist (Puar and Rai) and Sikhs have been the victims of a significant amount of hate crimes (Sidhu and Gohil).

Within this context of marginalization and confrontation with the prevailing hegemonic culture, the mother's role, as being responsible for the religious socialization of her children, becomes highly politicized. Mothering is a site for resistance to the prevailing forms of racism and many mothers advocate for their children, regardless of their religious, cultural and racial background. For Sikh mothers this advocacy takes on a deeper meaning—that of a decolonizing practice. In this study some of the mothers would visit their child's school to give presentations on *Sikhi* and/or about anti-racism, inclusion and difference. Another example of advocacy is the children's picture book, "*A Lion's Mane*," written by Navjot Kaur (2009). These mothers are not merely advocating for their child's well being but rather have a larger impact on the school community and beyond.

Sikh mothers clearly demonstrate forms of empowered mothering in their daily lives. Along with maternal agency, authority, autonomy and

authenticity I have added the concept of advocacy as a defining charac-
teristic of empowered Sikh mothering. Sikh mothering includes all five
characteristics in making a difference, not only in the lives of their own
children nor solely for Sikh children but for *all* children as we move
towards a different and better world.

ENDNOTES

[1]*Kesh*: hair.

[2]*Dastaar*: carefully tied turban.

[3]*Sangat*: gathering of Sikhs.

[4]For an in depth introduction to *Sikhi*, see the work of Singh, N. (2011).

[5]*Sati* refers to the self-immolation of a widow on her husband's funeral
pyre. For more detailed information see Major; Datta.

[6]*Khalsa*: meaning is pure.

[7]The words "*Kaur*" (meaning: princess or lioness) and "*Singh*" (meaning:
lion) are significant in the Sikh community. Guru Gobind Singh bestowed
these names, to be used as middle names or surnames on Sikh women
and men to further reinforce the equality of women in Sikhism, eliminate
caste hierarchies, and express how Sikhs were advocates for social justice.

[8]A *sevay-daar* literally translates into "servant who serves selflessly."

[9]*Keshdhari* is literally someone who bears *kesh*.

[10]*Gurudwara:* literally means "doorway to the Guru" and refers to the
Sikh place of worship.

[11]*Kirtan:* singing of the Guru's compositions.

[12]*Gursikh*: This term refers to Sikhs who have been initiated into the *Khalsa*.
The *Khalsa* refers to Sikhs who have been baptized through the *Amrit*
ceremony created by Guru Gobind Singh, the tenth Sikh Guru in 1699.

[13]*Gurmat*: the Guru's wisdom.

[14]*Amritdhari:* one who possesses *Amrit*. A devout Sikh.

[15]*Keshki*: material covering the *kesh*. The *keshki* is a small *dastaar*.

[16]*Gurbani*: words that are written in the Sikh Holy Book the *Guru
Granth Sahib*.

[17]*Bani* is a short form for *Gurbani*.

WORKS CITED

Attride-Stirling, J. "Thematic Networks: an Analytic Tool for Qualitative
Research." *Qualitative Research* 1.3 (2001): 385-405. Print.

Aulakh, Raveena. "A Sikh's Cost of Fitting In: Lopping off Long Hair." *The Toronto Star* 19 May 2009. Accessed 1 July 2010. Web.

Bhachu, Parminder. Dangerous Designs: Asian Women Fashion the Diaspora Economies. New York: Routledge, 2004. Print.

Brah, Avtar. Cartographies of Diaspora: Contesting Identities. London: Routledge, 1996. Print.

Braun, Virginia, and Victoria Clarke. "Using Thematic Analysis in Psychology." *Qualitative Research in Psychology* 3.2 (2006): 77-101. Print.

Datta, V. N. *Sati: A Historical, Social and Philosophical Inquiry into the Hindu Rite of Widow Burning*. New Delhi: Manohar. 1988. Print.

Klassen, Robert M. and George K. Georgiou. "Spelling and Writing Self-efficacy of Indo-Canadian and Anglo-Canadian Early Adolescents." *Journal of International Migration and Integration* 9.3 (2008): 311-26. Print.

Major, Andrea. *Sati: A Historical Anthology*. New Delhi: Oxford University Press. 2007. Print.

Nabha, Kahn Singh. *Gur Shabad Ratanakar Mahankosh*. Amritsar: Sudarshan, 1930. Print.

O'Reilly, Andrea. *From Motherhood to Mothering: the Legacy of Adrienne Rich's* Of Woman Born. Albany: State University of New York, 2004. Print.

Puar, J. K. and Rai, A. S. "Monster, Terrorist, Fag: The War on Terrorism and the Production of Docile Patriots." *Social Text* 20.3 72 (2002): 117-48. Print.

Sidhu, Dawinder S. and Neha Singh Gohil. "The Sikh Turban: Post-9/11 Challenges to this Article of Faith." *Rutgers Journal of Law and Religion* 9 (2008): 10-18.

Sikh Coalition. "Hatred in the Hallways." *The Sikh Coalition*. 6 June 2007. Web. 02 Aug. 2010.

Singh, Nikky-Guninder Kaur. *The Feminine Principle in the Sikh Vision of the Transcendent*. Cambridge: Cambridge University Press, 1993. Print.

Singh, Nikky-Guninder Kaur. *Sikhism: An Introduction*. London: I. B. Tauris, 2011. Print.

Singh, Pashaura "Early Markers of Sikh Identity." *Sikh Identity: Continuity and Change*. Ed. Pashaura Singh and N. Gerald Barrier. New Delhi: Manohar, 1999. Print.

Verma, Rita. "Trauma, Cultural Survival and Identity Politics in a Post-9/11 Era: Reflections by Sikh Youth." *Sikh Formations: Religion, Culture, Theory* 2.1 (2006): 89-101. Print.

The Fires of Transformation

JASJIT K. SANGHA

When our tendency to blame circumstances, people and other imaginary sources of pain reaches its height, and we are completely frustrated, we are finally forced to turn within. When suffering reaches its extreme, we turn upon our inner psyche to discover that the source of our pain is self-created. At this point, we are ready to learn, to inquire, to explore ourselves sincerely and become capable of self-reflection and self-transcendence. Then we determine our destiny, and create the world we wish to live in from the inside out.

—Mangala Anshumati (2009)

M Y THROAT IS PARCHED and burning. My head throbs. I am emotionally exhausted. A tsunami of anger welled up in me and once it started I couldn't hold it back. I look up at my stepdaughter who has stood in the same spot for over an hour, blank-faced, not even flinching. She is like a rock—hard, rigid and impossible to move.

My neighbour appears in my doorway. He looks disgusted.

"Can you please keep your voices down? I don't like all this yelling."

"Yeah, sure—sorry about that."

I want to tell him that I am finished being angry, that I am not usually like this, that I was pushed to the limits of my patience and understanding. But, instead, I shut the door and head upstairs. There is nothing left for me to say to my stepdaughter.

I check on my children. They are huddled together under the blankets on my son's bed. I hold them tightly in my arms and kiss their soft cheeks.

"I don't want to grow up, Mommy."

"I don't want to be a teenager."

I am speechless. I stroke their soft hair. I hate the person I become when I react to my stepdaughter, and I am perplexed as to how to change my behaviour. With my limitations, it feels impossible for me to me to give her my love, even though she is at a time in her life when she needs it most.

I hold my children tighter and find solace in their responsive hugs and kisses.

*

When I acted out as a teenager, my parents did not know what to do with me. In their hometowns, nestled in the lush green flatlands of Punjab, teenagers from respectable families did not behave in self-destructive or unpredictable ways. They were too busy studying for college entrance exams and maintaining their reputations for future marriage prospects. In my parents' generation, young people relied on older family members to help them make decisions about their lives. The dreams of their parents, grandparents and extended family paved the road that they followed. This was especially directed towards the girls, for whom there was great pressure to uphold the honour of the family. Staying out late, dating, experimenting with drugs and alcohol—the defining characteristics of many North American teens—was unheard of for them. This made me an anomaly in my family—but just another kid in my peer group. Part of my confusion stemmed from experiencing racism outside the home yet feeling suffocated by my family's cultural expectations inside the home. I felt isolated, torn, and guilty at times, but my friends swayed me away from my parents and their values with the lure of thrills and late-night adventures.

I thought I understood this teenage angst when my stepdaughters faced similar problems but my anger often got in the way of my understanding. Instead of having compassion, and remembering how hard that period of time was in my own life, I wanted obedience. My relationship with my husband dwindled into one long argument with no beginning or end. I wanted him to parent in a way that I knew and understood according to my culture; he wanted to follow his instincts about what his daughters needed.

My husband was not afraid of the chaos associated with adolescence. He was raised in an environment where non-conformity and the questioning of authority were commonplace. The early part of his life was spent living communally in rural Saskatchewan amongst expansive wheat fields, under an enormous blue sky. His mother "dropped out" of society with a group of young, idealistic friends, creating an anti-establishment haven where free love prevailed. The experiment fell apart when he was school-aged and his mother raised him and his sister on her own—at times living communally with other women. By the time he was a teenager he had experienced generous amounts of freedom and independence. He had the life skills to tend to his own needs and the maturity to take care of his newborn daughter at the age of 16.

When my stepdaughters entered adolescence my husband focused on maintaining his relationships with them. He worried about them, but showed them respect. Anger festered inside me when I heard him speaking calmly to them when they came home hours after their curfew or brought home a failing report card. I became really upset if their surliness was directed towards the younger children. I caused myself much anguish trying to change them, just as I had when they were younger, but this time it was so much worse. Their wills were strong and they had no interest in appeasing me.

Before long, I had a ball of anxiety firmly wedged in my gut. Home no longer provided consolation after a long day, and I dreaded the weekends because struggles over curfews were the most intense. My husband could see embers of hostility flickering in my eyes and avoided engaging me in conversation. As circumstances grew increasingly difficult I struggled to find the inner peace and guidance I had cultivated through my spiritual practice. It seemed to come so naturally when life was less challenging. When the situation became unbearable, I sought to understand the source of my anger and leaned on the *satsanga* to help me find meaning.

*

The sun warms my shoulders, and I watch the waves crash on the shore. The smell and sound of the water soothes me. The tension in my head eases as the wind blows off the water and brushes against me. I want to enjoy this moment with my husband and children, but instead, he and I return to the same old argument about my younger stepdaughter.

"So, what are you going to do about it?" I demand to know.

"Nothing," he says.

"What do you mean, 'nothing'?"

"There's nothing I can do."

"So, you're saying that we just have to sit back and watch while she does god knows what, and forgive her every time?"

"Yes," he says.

"Why?"

"Because we're parents. We're the adults, and we have to do that for her."

The tension in my head returns. I am so tired of being angry all the time. I get up and start to walk along the beach hoping to find some relief from my frustration. The words of my spiritual teacher Mangala Anshumati drift into my heart, "Love is a powerful force—honest, respectful and compelling—whereas physical or psychological manipulation and control are damaging and ineffective. If we hope to guide our children in every moment, we need to steer them by the gentle hand of love" (Anshumati 2012).

*

I drive past the city limits into the green, rolling hills and solitude of the country, and feel a sense of peace slowly descending upon me. I set up my meditation pillow on the back lawn of the house where I gather with my spiritual community. I close my eyes and sink slowly into my surroundings. My spiritual teacher does not start her talk until the satsanga has gathered together, performed kirtan and meditated for some time. These opening practices create a feeling of stillness and receptivity, drawing people away from their minds and into their hearts. The wind blows through the trees and the smell of rain hangs in the air as my spiritual teacher speaks, "Meditation is not a religious practice. It is a natural human ability, where you function from the core of your pure intelligence and awareness. Seated meditation is only a preparation for the practice of conscious living in every moment.

"The more you practice meditation, the more you are able to rise above the pain and suffering of life. This potential is not limited by any difference in your intelligence, personality or constitution, but simply depends upon your ability to learn to go beyond the mind."

I ask her a question—hoping for a reassuring answer.

"Can we ease the suffering of our children?"

She turns her attention to me.

"Ultimately, you cannot make your children happy, and it is not your responsibility. All you can do is respectfully guide them, offer unconditional love, and demonstrate your love in a way that they can understand."

I begin to sob heavily, feeling my body overcome with sadness.

She continues, compassionately, "Though we cannot completely take away our children's suffering, if we focus upon our spirituality, the benefits spill over to our children. The blessings of all our positive actions naturally extend toward our family. Living an enlightened life of truth and service is the greatest thing we can ever do to ensure our children's protection and happiness" (Anshumati 2006).

*

I sit down to meditate, praying for understanding. I want the tears to flow and give me some relief from the tension that is spreading through my body. I close my eyes and feel tears stream down my face. My body relaxes for the first time in days, and my breathing returns to an even and steady rhythm. My eyes are closed, but I see brightness in the room. My body feels warm, as though it is wrapped in a gentle embrace. I see the face of my spiritual teacher laughing with joy and I begin to laugh also. My worries seem far away.

*

Through a regular practice of meditation and an ongoing relationship to my *satsanga* I uncovered some hard truths about myself. The anger that consumed me, threatening to destroy my relationship with my stepdaughters, had nothing to do with them and everything to do with me. Their behaviour merely brought my own unresolved feelings to the surface. The harder I tried to resist these feelings, the more antagonistic I was with my stepdaughters.

My anger was so powerful that it covered up how I was really feeling, prolonging its hold on me. I discovered a huge well of sadness underneath my anger. I was sad and disappointed that my stepdaughters did not follow the path that I had imagined for them and I felt responsible for their lives. I remembered them as little girls wearing mismatched clothes and running around the house carefree. I also felt sadness—and shock—at how quickly they grew up, towering over me. I never really had a chance to develop the kind of relationship I wanted to have with them. Feeling this sadness made me more appreciative of my own mother's struggle with me, and her initial shock and sadness around my life choices.

The hardest part of my anger was acknowledging and accepting that I was envious of their freedom. I wanted to come and go as I pleased in the house without expectations from the whole family that I be dependable and responsible. I knew I could not show up five minutes before dinner and have a hot meal ready for me on the table, or hide in my room for the evening because I was feeling low. Unlike my stepdaughters, I did not have the freedom to make mistakes or be given the benefit of a doubt.

I was an adult and a mother. I was expected to behave in a certain way to maintain my respectability. My stepdaughters did not carry that burden. They had the freedom to make wrong turns and be guided back to a path of safety by the adults around them. The responsibilities of life were slowly encroaching on their consciousness, while I was wading thigh-high in the thicket of life.

Meanwhile my freedom was being curtailed even further. In order to maintain a relationship with the girls I needed to evolve more as a person. Although self-transformation was a step forward, I hated change and, especially, hated changing myself. But in order to fully face my anger, and to salvage my family relationships, it was necessary.

*

I sit on my pillow in meditation class, happy and at peace. The complex emotions surrounding my home situation blissfully fade away in the company of my spiritual teacher. Her talk on emotions brings me clarity about my own life. I ask her a question.

"When I feel angry, it just washes over me, almost controlling me."

She nods.

"How can I change that?"

"Allow yourself to feel your anger fully—and feel whatever else arises within you—without any resistance."

I listen trying to process her words.

"Your emotion will eventually pass, but the actions you take while you are angry have lasting consequences. By giving yourself the freedom to feel your emotions completely, you allow yourself more room to explore what is underneath them and more time to consider the actions you will take. Don't be afraid of your thoughts and feelings, they are temporary, but your actions are more permanent. As a fully conscious being, you are able to see the consequences of your actions even before they are committed" (Anshumati 2005).

My heart sinks. I have reacted harshly in anger too many times.

*

My husband sits on the edge of my bed, waiting for me to change my mind.

"You are asking me to do the hardest thing in the world right now," I say.

He nods his head. I sigh.

"Okay, I'll go in there and talk to her."

He rubs my back for a moment then leaves the room. I slowly get up

67

off the bed and cross the hall to my stepdaughter's room. Anxiety fills my stomach. The tension between her and me has been building for weeks. She is lying in bed, with the light off. I touch her shoulder gently.

"Are you awake?

She rolls over to look at me. We struggle to see each other in the dark. I take a deep breath.

"I just want you to know that I love you."

I reach over to her and give her a hug.

*

My daughter's high-pitched laughter echoes down the hall. She runs out of her bedroom and down the stairs with her brother chasing her. His screams are getting louder and louder.

"Give me back my car! Give me back my car!"

My daughter grabs my shirt and runs behind me, continuing to laugh as she teases her brother. He keeps screaming.

"I want my car!"

My son grabs at his sister as I stand between the two of them. My head starts to feel hot as anger rises within me. I am on the verge of exploding as the familiar sensation of frustration encapsulates me. My hands reach out to grab my children's arms to break up the fight, but I manage to stop myself. Instead, I move away from them, take a few breaths and pour myself a glass of cold water. The moment passes and my anger retreats.

*

The more I understood my anger the less willing I was to let it interfere with my relationships. It still reared its ugly head at inappropriate times but it did not control me. I started to see my anger as a signal that I was unhappy with something. In order to overcome it, I needed to sit with myself and understand my needs better. It was a refreshing change from always thinking that somebody else was making me angry, that it was their fault I was feeling agitated. The more I deciphered my own feelings the better I empathized with my stepdaughters, and sought moments of connection with them.

When I invited them, without judgment, to share what was happening in their lives, they readily opened up. We talked about what was happening with their friends, choices they were making, who they were dating, and the visions they had for their futures. My relationships with them were not perfect—they still closed up at times, and so did I—but there was an upswing in our relationship. Although my ego was often pummeled, it was liberating to feel connection again—both with the girls and with myself.

My new feeling of openness trickled down to the rest of the family. The tension between my husband and I began to dissolve as my relationships with our children improved. I found a way to communicate without spiraling into accusations, blame or criticism. Being able to express myself more often and more effectively restored a feeling of closeness between us. I had really taken to heart the guidance of Mangala Anshumati, "To communicate effectively with your children, keep your voice calm, respectful and without undertones, or your words may have the opposite effect of what you had hoped for. To preserve the intimacy and trust of the relationship with your children, maintain your intention to only do and say things that will make the situation better" (Anshumati 2012). My children marveled at my calm and subdued reactions to their pranks or bickering. I was more aware of their emotions, and that look on their faces when my words or actions stabbed their fragile hearts.

By beginning to understand my anger, I had the freedom I longed for—to contemplate my own needs and how I wanted to live my life.

This chapter is reprinted with permission, from Stepmothering: A Spiritual Journey, *by J. K. Sangha (Bradford: Demeter Press, 2012).*

WORKS CITED

Anshumati, Mangala. "Meditation." Class Talk and Q&A. CFCA, Uxbridge, Sept. 2006.

Anshumati, Mangala. "Pain and Suffering Turns Us Within." Informal Talk. Toronto, April 2009.

Anshumati, Mangala. "Raising Children Who Are Free." Class Talk and Q&A. CFCA, Uxbridge, August. 2005.

Anshumati, Mangala. "Spiritual Mothering." In-progress title. Unpublished Manuscript. Toronto, 2012.

South Asian Activist Mothers Speak Out About Politics, Sexuality and Health

JASJIT K. SANGHA AND TAHIRA GONSALVES

MOTHERING can be a form of empowerment for women—despite constraints imposed on their lives—through everyday acts of resistance they engage in while raising their children (Porter). For the South Asian activist mothers we interviewed for this chapter, everyday acts of resistance are embedded in their lives through their relationships with their children, their work and their engagement with wider society. They struggle to shield their children from oppression by creating a "homeplace" in which they can restore their dignity, as well as through challenging social institutions, government policies, and raising public awareness (hooks). In this way, their motherwork centres around issues of social justice, critical thinking and resistance, in a socio-political context of marginalization. Their activism is both private and public, and for them, mothering truly is a political act. Through this chapter we will highlight the main themes that emerged from our interview with these dynamic women to show how they participated in empowered mothering despite significant obstacles they faced in their daily lives stemming from: racial profiling of Muslims post 9/11, homophobia faced by same-sex families, and misunderstanding of rare health conditions.

In this chapter, we have intentionally chosen to give primacy to the voices of the women we interviewed through long verbatim quotes from them, with minimal analysis from us. Although we have not followed traditional academic conventions, this chapter is an important contribution to our understanding of mothering in the South Asian diaspora through a rich discussion of issues that are often deemed to be controversial. The chapter has been divided into four sections, based on the main themes that emerged from the interview: The activists become mothers, the mother becomes an activist; Muslim identity and racial profiling post 9/11; Forced vulnerability, "outing" and constant vigilance; and Resisting gender roles and nurturing resilience.

THE ACTIVISTS BECOME MOTHERS, THE MOTHER BECOMES AN ACTIVIST

The three women we interviewed were: Zohra (all names used in this chapter are pseudonyms), a political activist, whose Muslim background became an identity label, especially for her son, post 9/11; Priya, an activist whose sexual identity as a queer woman became more public after she had children; and Meera, a woman who was thrust into activism because of a rare health condition from which both her children suffer. We began by asking the women how they defined their own activism in relation to their identities and what influence this had on their mothering.

Zohra—To me mothering is being an activist; it's a political act, particularly when you are raising kids who are racialized, in western societies. And this is over and above the regular trials and tribulations of raising children and all the trauma that goes with it, in terms of negotiating values and social systems. I think ultimately as an immigrant mother, by definition, parenting is a political act. That to me is more of an example of innate activism than anything we choose to do or get paid for. I was an activist in my other life as well, but the kind of activism I have adopted here has very much to do with my children. In fact it's entirely motivated by my kids—I do it for them.

Priya—I was an activist long before I had kids, so I'd say in some ways my activism has informed my mothering rather than the opposite. Now it's starting to change and both are kind of integrated, but I see myself as someone who is politically active and trying to change the world to make it a better place for the kids and, personally, because of my politics as a socialist.

Meera—I have become an activist because I am a mother. It started because of the challenges in my personal life—my kids have a medical condition they were born with, so it sort of became a fight every single time there were health issues for them. So having no activist background, I had to start speaking up, fighting with people because of what they were being put through at different stages.

For all three women, activism and motherhood form inseparable aspects of their identities, irrespective of which came first in their lives. They all also reiterate how mothering has made them strong(er) activists, given that they felt they were fighting for their children.

MUSLIM IDENTITY AND RACIAL PROFILING POST 9/11

For Zohra and Meera, the terrorist attacks that occurred on 9/11 led to a turning point in their mothering experience. Prior to this, their religion was a personal set of beliefs that they expressed as they wished. After 9/11, they were forced to take on a public Muslim identity in the wake of increasing hatred directed towards Muslims. In this section they express the anxiety they felt as mothers of young Muslim boys, who seemed to bear the brunt of this public anger. They also share how they responded, as activists, to the unfair racial profiling of Muslims.

Zohra—9/11 is an incident that brought our Muslim identity to the forefront, I mean I've been here 23 years and it was never important when I first came, but suddenly after 9/11 my Muslim identity became more important, and of course it has a profoundly negative impact on my children more than myself. My son was pretty young at the time when 9/11 happened and soon he started getting into trouble in school. And it's not my daughter, it's my son. It's a very male thing. Young Muslim men are far more likely to suffer the consequences of people's understanding of what they think is happening in the world and what Muslims are all about.

My son went through some really really tough times. He was about twelve when this whole thing happened so he was just becoming politically conscious. A lot of my work also involved working with young Muslim kids who were getting into trouble in the school system. I was working at the time with a legal clinic, so a lot of cases used to come to us around young kids getting into trouble at the school. Minor incidents turning into major suspensions; all kinds of innuendos and allegations about children and families and parents having anxiety because suddenly their child who used to be at the top of the class is now being threatened with suspension for the whole year or something. So, I remember a couple of times, having to intervene as a parent advocate on behalf of the parents. And it wasn't just Muslims. I remember working with a non-Muslim family whose child was being targeted because his friends were Muslim.

All kinds of strange things were happening so that kind of defined the environment in which we functioned.

Zohra experienced this period from the perspectives of both her daughter and son, and this brought out for her, the gendered ways in which 9/11 impacted Muslims. For Meera, her experience as a Muslim had always been as a minority, even in her home country of India, prior to immigration.

Meera—Well, we've always lived in a place where politically, there were upheavals going on between major [Hindu] and minor [Muslim] communities and we were the only minority family—but we had a lot of protection there [in our neighbourhood in India]. Even from the majority families, our neighbours always used to be looking out for us even though we were the only minority family living in that particular location. But it always used to make us feel vulnerable, scared, especially having eight kids in the home—six girls and just two boys. We were always scared for the safety of the girls. Here, after 9/11 things sort of totally changed and it's been very scary.... I just can't put it into words how much fear I felt for my kids and my family.

When we see the way politics target and treat people who are Muslim and show it, rather than hiding it, and then sometimes they are connected to terrorism and then the way things go downhill for those families. It's very hard. I worry about my kids and my family. We are very moderate. My family has always been working with the community for access to education, social supports, etc. But it always scares me, that if anyone points a finger and accuses you, how do you come back into society, how to you stay connected and not have to move away?

Both Zohra and Meera reveal the very real consequences of racial profiling on Muslims and the sense of fear this has produced for Muslim mothers. Although as activists, they have been able to address some cases of discrimination that are taking place in the education system, the intensity of Islamaphobia is pervasive.

FORCED VULNERABILITY, "OUTING," AND CONSTANT VIGILANCE

In this section, all three mothers highlight how the public meaning attached to their personal identities leads to a vulnerability that is forced or imposed upon them, and their children. This in turn has consequences on their children's sense of self. In order to buffer the effects of the subordination their children may experience, the mothers are constantly being vigilant for instances when it happens, so they can address it.

Zohra—I'm not exactly a Muslim activist. But when you live in environments like these or any other where some part of your identity is being used to undermine your kids, as a mother it has an impact on you. The family supports are there, but it's the Muslim identity after 9/11 that has really made me vulnerable towards my kids. Because you know I can take a lot of shit myself, but I will not allow my kids to suffer. Now they are older, they can take care of themselves. But this has been going on for a while. It takes its toll.

I watched my son's anger as he's growing up, talking about, 'why is it that they hate us so much?' And then hating all those people that have done terrible things in the name of Islam so he has to suffer the consequences. The question is how to teach your children: not to hate themselves, not to blame yourself, and not to blame someone else? How do we deal with the contradictions—other people can do bad things but the whole race or the whole group should not be maligned. But you feel responsible anyway.

His identity became so conflated with everything negative, to a point where my son stopped meeting anyone but Muslim kids. His rationale was: 'because I don't have to explain myself!' He doesn't have to explain or stop and give a political analysis of America's foreign policy, which is what got him into trouble in the first place in school. So I can understand his reasoning entirely, but as a mother it also makes you vulnerable. If it was just his baggy pants and his girlfriend and his school grades, those I could handle. But it's not knowing … when he is playing basketball and you don't know where he is and you don't know who he's hanging out with and you don't know how the police is going to see him.

He recently went abroad—to a Muslim country—in the first year of University to do his internship at a pharmaceutical company. Four months later he's travelling back and about a week before he's coming I wake up in the middle of the night sweating. I'm thinking, "oh, my god" here is a 19-20 year old kid, he's a kid of Muslim origin, he's coming back from a Muslim country after spending four months working in a pharmaceutical company. And if I know him—he hasn't shaved and he's travelling. Oh my god, he fits the worst profile! I mean do you think they'll believe he worked in a legitimate place? Even if they believe he worked for a pharmaceutical company do you think they'll believe he just did it as an internship? And at the airport sure enough he was the last one to come out, but he did come out. And sure enough they questioned him; they asked him for proof that he had done his internship. Thank god I had told him to get a letter from the company. I asked him to keep a copy of his final report, keep a letter from the managing director saying that he worked there and this is what his duties were, showing that he was not making a bomb.... And sure enough they asked him every single thing.

Those kinds of things make you vulnerable and, to me, that's also violence against women, because it makes you paranoid, it makes you constantly second guess yourself, constantly be more vigilant than anybody else. And then having to work on your kids to make sure they feel strong within—to withstand the prejudice/racism outside and that they don't either end up hating society, or end up hating who they are, or internalize all the hatred and end up violating themselves because they can't live with it. I think that is over and above the call of duty called motherhood. No parenting should be about that.

For Priya, this forced vulnerability does not have to do with being a Muslim, but because she is a queer mother. She constantly has to "out" her sexual identity when she is in public spaces with her children due to questions she receives from complete strangers. As a result she has to continuously be watchful for occurrences of homophobia directed towards herself or her children.

Priya—As a lesbian, moving here when I was 16 and being very active in politics from the age of 17 I had never thought I'd have children. Especially coming out as a lesbian when I was 21, it was sort of something I would have never even thought of. Part of my work has been about trying to help support organizations, coalitions and networks to come together to fight for social justice or against racism. These are projects that I've been working on for decades. But my sexual identity was my own private business before I had children. I could be in the world and nobody would ask any questions.

But once you become a mother a whole bunch of you becomes exposed. My sexual identity is not something I've ever wanted to be in the forefront of organizing around. There are people who do it and I commend them for doing it, but it's not my thing. I'm not an extrovert around my sexuality, my identity; I don't need to tell everyone I'm a lesbian. But being a mother has made me come out everywhere, I don't have a choice about it. My sexual identity is like ding! I might as well tattoo 'Lesbian' on my forehead you know, because it's out there and I have to be out and proud because of my kids. I don't want to be out and proud half the time, I just want to go buy my groceries, or go to the park, or get a coffee, or walk the dog....

When you then have kids, as a lesbian, you are negotiating with the child care system, school, institutions.... And with people on the street who feel like they have the license to look at your family and make all kinds of comments and ask you all kinds of questions that they would never think of ever asking a straight couple. And so it leads you to negotiating the world in a different way. I'm trying to figure it out because there aren't many of us who are going through this. So I'm trying to negotiate this everyday so that my kids don't feel ashamed of the color of their skin and who they are but also that they don't feel ashamed of being kids of lesbians and also having some connection to this South Asian community that doesn't want to have anything to do with them. And then that's in addition to making sure the child care system, the school system, everywhere, the neighbours, everyone around them is going to be cool with them and so I fight for them, my partner and I fight for them every day so they can be okay in the world as they are.

And that's just a layer of work that goes on everywhere.... It's just something that's part of your day, in terms of interacting. Just even taking the dog for a walk you deal with it. And I know people are just not aware and they're just coming from their own heterosexual assumptions, but it's the combination of them assuming I'm heterosexual and then making comments in front of the kids. Sometimes it's just like unbelievable the shit that people will say to you. "How many times did you inseminate to have your kids?" I'm like, do I say to you, "How many times did you have sex with your husband before you got pregnant?" And it's just constant in terms of what you have to deal with.

Meera—The sort of struggles you're talking about—I've seen quite a bit of those kinds of things but it's not in relation to sexuality, but in relation to my kids. They've got a genetic skin condition which one child in a few hundred thousand will have. When we lived in India, no one could even diagnose what it was, but I was very persistent and had great doctors who were able to explain to me, and that helped me figure out how to deal with it. With this condition you know you can't kiss your kid—they get a blister. You could give them a hug and then they'll have something happening on their skin. So to deal with that every single day, it used to be a big struggle. In school, the sort of bullying they experienced, especially my son—kids can be the most cruel, right. There was a time when my two-and-a-half year old daughter went to school covered in bandages because she had a crop of blisters. The wounds needed to be covered to prevent infections from setting in. So I sent my daughter to school and she was sent out to the principal's office by her teacher. This happened in spite of the school knowing that it was not infectious.

The principal actually pointed to her face and said that my daughter was not fit for the school. I was hopping mad! So I got a letter from the doctor that said that she's okay. And that sort of totally changed me, what was happening with the kids. Anytime I stepped out of the house, I would be asked, "oh, did you do this in your pregnancy, or when they were born did you do this or did you do that?" So, I never used to speak. I was a very anti-social person, but that sort of experience made me very protective of my kids to make sure that no one could ever hurt them. I had to take care of it myself because doctors wanted me to be self-sufficient. I had to learn to treat their blisters and give them their needles. So there is one part of you that is trying to deal with society and there's the other part that still has to take care of the kids when they are crying. And the kids have dealt with their own emotional baggage. Today it just makes me very proud of them when I see what they have achieved, despite everything.

All three mothers have become stronger and more vocal, despite feeling vulnerable, in order to address attempts to disempower or censure them or their children. They feel empathy for their children who have been exposed to hurtful stereotypes, at a very young age, and try to create spaces for them strengthen their selfhood.

RESISTING GENDER ROLES AND NURTURING RESILIENCE

While all three mothers are fiercely protective of their children, they have also encouraged their children to be independent, critical thinkers, who challenge and resist gender stereotypes, conservatism and inequity. In this section they speak about their practice of mothering, and why these values are important to them.

Priya—I think that before I had kids, when I was pregnant I had all these images and notions of what I was going to be like and now I have learned to be a bit more relaxed about it. I mean I've never bought them Barbie dolls, but at one point my little one said, "my friends have hundreds of Barbie dolls, why don't I have any?" And I told a few of her aunties and she got a few Barbie dolls. I just feel like they've got so much working against them in some ways, and so we as parents need to teach them to just ask lots of questions, I want to help them to become critical thinkers, have conversations about issues. So, if she wants Barbie dolls, or to dress in pink all day, or if she wants to grow her hair long or whatever it is—that's okay.

Zohra—I thought it was so ridiculous that when my son was born he had to be in blue and my daughter had to be in pink, and I thought, "you call yourself liberated [in Western society] you're so tied to gender roles that it makes no sense." So I used to dress my son in purple and my daughter in blue. I find certain overt symbols of feminism to be so passé. At school when my daughter beats all the nerds at Calculus and Chemistry and she's getting 90 percent and she's wearing her high heels—she feels good! You see, that's what makes her feel real. To me that's true empowerment and all on her terms. It's not about the superficial symbols like how you dress.

If we are teaching our kids equity and empowerment, that's a whole different ballgame, that's a whole different conversation. I agree it has to do with critical thinking, just as I had to teach my kids to be Muslims and not hate themselves, not hate the world, be proud, still be able to tell the difference between right and wrong and fight bigotry when they see it, be it against Muslims or anyone else.

I have to teach them about gender as well. I remember when my son, after 9/11, started going to Friday prayers, which I thought was very peculiar because never before had he shown any signs of going to Friday prayers. And I told him, 'If you're going for Friday prayers because it gives you some personal space, some spiritual comfort that's great. I think it's marvelous. But if you're going and then two days later you are going to come and tell me and your sister how we should be behaving or dressing and what your prayers and salvation mean in terms of us—"I will come down hard on you. You know that right?" Two weeks later he stopped going to Friday prayers.

I asked him why he wasn't going and he told me, "They are talking nonsense." A young kid from high school would stand there and give a so-called sermon and he would say irrelevant things and make their friends—who were women—stand at the back and not next to them to pray. So he stopped going. It wasn't only the prayer that was important, but it was the socialization piece as well. And the ability to think it through—that my faith does not have to be tied to these symbolisms of marginalizing Muslim women and then calling myself a good Muslim. If it means I don't go to Friday Prayers with you then so be it. And I have more respect for my son for taking that stance than any feminist discourse I may have had with him. He looked at the whole thing and thought my mom and my sister would never put up with this and I would never do this to them.

Priya—See, that would be my goal: to have my kids be able to make those decisions and feel very good in themselves about doing that. I think, I have two girls and so I deal with a lot of the girl culture and as you know it can be pretty judgmental and nasty. I think that's where we try and intervene and ask lots of questions. And in some ways we are helping them choose friends that are coming from families that are open about girls being girls, and being the best they can be, but again being critical thinkers, but not try to prescribe it for them, but let them explore it themselves a little bit. And make mistakes—that's the thing.

For the activist mothers, an important part of their mothering was raising their children with a strong sense of equity and social justice. They provided guidance and advice when needed. But they also understood that their children would really have to learn the true meaning of these values themselves, through their own experiences in the world.

FINAL THOUGHTS FROM ACTIVIST MOTHERS

For these women, mothering has left an indelible mark on their lives and their work by transforming who they are, and how they relate to their activism. This section captures their final thoughts on being an activist and a mother.

Meera—Kids, they totally make our lives, for South Asian moms we feel a purpose because of our kids. But even before kids, it's childbirth, God has given us the experience of childbirth which totally makes you a different person.

Zohra—Parenting is about transformation. I think we get transformed. If I didn't have kids I would have been a different person. That's not to say I wouldn't be political, but my politics would have a very different angle to it. I think the kind of politics I have now has a lot to do with the fact that I'm a mother and I have kids and their consideration makes me a different kind of activist and I prefer this—I like this. It's less individualistic; it's more collective it's more cohesive—less dogmatic, more forgiving. It makes you humble.

Priya—I think especially when you do activist work it takes a toll and you see a lot of rough stuff every day, but I think you can't take that home. But we need to be able to explain things and why it is important to go to this demonstration and why we are going to that rally. You have to talk about it and explain the relevance in their lives. So I think now is the time to keep explaining and stay optimistic. Some people I see say, "Oh, what's the point?" When you have kids you have to say, "No, there is a point."

CONCLUSION

Zohra, Priya, and Meera are three ordinary, yet extraordinary women, carrying on their mothering in sometimes very difficult circumstances. Their resilience and struggles speak to the commonality of their situations with that of other immigrant and racialized women, but also to the tremendous resistance and power that these women can and do show. While all three mothers are members of "marginalized" groups, their marginalization does not take away from the ways in which they've carved spaces and practices that are empowering for themselves and their children. They have done this by pushing back against attempts to silence or subordinate them or their children and cultivating a homeplace that sustains them despite the regular onslaught of demoralization they experience (hooks 267).

Zohra does this by leaving open spaces for her daughter to be a feminist on her own terms, and for her son to navigate being a young Muslim man in his own way. Priya does this by allowing the intersections of her politics, her queer identity and her South Asian heritage to shape her mothering practice. And Meera has done this with a quiet and unassuming strength, working to protect and promote her children's well-being.

Their stories show how the process of mothering—in a society that negates people's identities due to their race, religion, sexuality or health—is a political act. It is not easy and is marked by feelings of vulnerability, fear and anxiety. However, as these South Asian mothers show, it is through everyday acts of resistance that this negation is challenged and these identities, for mothers and their children, are validated.

WORKS CITED

hooks, b. "Homeplace: A Site of Resistance." *Maternal Theory Essential Readings*. Ed. A. O'Reilly. Toronto: Demeter Press. 2007. 266-273. Print.

O'Reilly, A. "Feminist Mothering." *Maternal Theory Essential Readings*. Ed. A. O'Reilly. Toronto: Demeter Press. 2007. 792-821. Print.

Porter, M. "Down Under Power? Australian Mothering Experiences in the 1950s, 1960s." *Motherhood: Power and Oppression*. Ed. M. Porter, P. Short and A. O'Reilly. Toronto: Women's Press. 2005. 181-193. Print.

Mothering, Mental Health and Well-Being

New Mothers in a New Land

The First Time Mothering Experiences
of Sri Lankan Tamils

SOUMIA MEIYAPPAN AND LYNNE LOHFELD

PREGNANCY AND CHILDBIRTH are life-altering experiences for most first time mothers. For Tamil newcomer[1] women these changes are even more pronounced as they undergo the resettlement and integration process in a new country. In addition to the emotional upheaval of leaving their home country, family and community behind after living through many years of a civil war, they also face the additional stress (albeit often a welcomed one) of becoming a new parent. Attempts to balance the loss of familiar ways of life with adoption of new ones may be particularly stressful for them. Not only are they physiologically vulnerable to emotional stress following birth, but they are also at the center of a cultural conflict—how to follow age-old postpartum practices without the support offered by knowledgeable family and community members. The lack of such supports places first-time newcomer mothers at increased risk for such mental health disorders as depression (Stewart et al. 123), which may be expounded due to culturally inappropriate or insufficient responses from the health care system in their receiving country (Hilton et al. 554).

Sri Lankan Tamils are among the fastest growing migrant groups in Canada. The Sri Lankan civil war (1983-2009) resulted in over one million Tamils fleeing their homeland, and over 250,000 Sri Lankan Tamils have settled in the Greater Toronto Area in Canada—the majority of whom came as immigrants or refugees (Guruge and Collins 236). Despite their large numbers in Canada, Tamil newcomer women are noticeably missing from the literature on migrant women's needs as new mothers. Given the potentially large number of women in these communities who are at elevated risk for health problems associated with both new mother and newcomer status, this issue can be seen as an important public health concern.

Before practices and policies to better meet the needs of Tamil-Canadian immigrant and refugee women in Toronto can be developed and enacted, the experiences of these women, from their own perspectives, must be elucidated. The women in our study are similar to immigrant and refugee women from other countries in their experiences of isolation and adjustment as new mothers in a new country. For example, one study exploring the narratives of immigrant Thai women in Australia who had become mothers found that these women faced a number of concerns in their new country, including: social isolation, different childrearing practices, and the desire to preserve Thai culture, which played an important role in their coping with motherhood (Liamputtong and Naksook 665).

However, unlike other studies with new immigrant mothers who came from war-torn countries, the Tamil mothers we interviewed were silent about their experiences with the war. For instance, in a study on refugee women's experiences of war and dislocation in the former Yugoslavia, researchers found that the "sense of disbelief, of the inconceivability of war between people who lived together, was echoed again and again" in their narratives (Wilcke 6). Even though the war in Sri Lanka was similarly devastating, the women in our study chose not to speak about the civil war they had lived through. Despite the fact that women in this study were not willing to break their silence about their experiences with war—and how that may have influenced their mental health—they were more open about the stresses they were facing as new mothers.

In this way, this study makes an important contribution to the literature through bringing forth the often silenced voices of newcomer Tamil mothers and attempting to gain an in-depth understanding of their first time mothering experiences. Instead of focusing on a clinical diagnosis for these mothers (i.e. post-partum depression) as is common in health care studies focussing on the mental health of new mothers (Ahmed, Stewart, Teng, Wahoush and Gagnon 295; Morrow et al. 594; Zelkowitz et al. 2), we are attempting to a attain a more nuanced understanding of their lives that explores how cultural and experiential factors influence their mental health. In this way, we hope to demonstrate the need for cultural competence and understanding as an important part of post-partum care for Tamil mothers.

METHODS

The qualitative research approach of hermeneutic phenomenology (HP) was chosen to explore this topic since the investigators were interested in understanding the meaning of the phenomenon—the first-time motherhood experience of Tamil immigrant and refugee women—in the participants own words (c.f. Gadamer). In this method, the researcher begins their study by identifying their own relevant understandings, experiences or "pre-understandings" of the phenomenon in reflexive journal entries. They then reflect on how their pre-understandings may influence their interpretation of the participants' experiences, prior to meeting with their participants. In HP it is important that the researcher remains aware of these pre-understandings, yet also remains open to the participants' points of view or *horizons* (one's perspective or vantage point, encompassing what one believes, has experienced and/or knows) as the researcher dialogues with participants during the individual interview, as well as with the resultant text (i.e. transcripts from these interviews).

The act of understanding and interpretation is then characterized by the intersection of two horizons—that of the researcher, and that of the participant, also termed as the *fusion of horizons* (Wilcke 4). At regular intervals throughout the study, researchers re-evaluate their initial understandings and refine them based on what they have heard or learned from the participants. As the goal of an HP study is to create a shared understanding and refined meaning of the experience of interest, it is important to fuse the researcher's initial and evolving horizon with the collective one developed through gaining a deep understanding and appreciation of the participants' horizons (Wilcke 4). Specifically, fusions of horizons is achieved through multiple cycles of speaking with the participants, reading transcripts of interviews, and reflecting on what the phenomenon could mean (Koch 835). The ultimate goal of carrying out such a study is to identify new *horizons of understanding*[2] of the phenomenon by incorporating both the researcher's understanding of this phenomenon and the participant's perspective.

As this project involved working with a specific group of immigrant and refugee women who may be difficult to access without community ties in the form of designated research partners drawn from their community, the investigators established a community advisory group, composed of Tamil-Canadian women from Toronto and service providers from settlement agencies. These individuals provided assistance with reviewing the data collection tools for appropriate and culturally sensitive wording, locating and recruiting participants and translating documents from English to Tamil and vice versa.

The following eligibility criteria were used to enrol participants in this study: a) having been born in Sri Lanka; b) being of Tamil origin; c) having migrated to Canada from Sri Lanka within the last ten years; d) currently living in the GTA; and e) having given birth to their first child in Canada. Eligible women were recruited by members of the community advisory group, with the aid of a flyer in Tamil that described the study and provided contact information for women to telephone a Tamil-speaking recruiter.

Individual interviews were carried out with each participant at her home, consisting of open-ended questions about life in Sri Lanka, migration to Canada, and the experience of becoming a new mother. Since this was a group that was relatively missing from the literature, we used open-ended questions in individual interviews, which allowed the women to talk about what they perceived to be most important or salient. A second interview was carried out with all but two of the participants to clarify any unclear statements made by the participants and to ask about any recommendations they had to offer for others, including service providers and other immigrant or refugee women.

FINDINGS

The study sample consisted of six women (26-35 years old). All of the women were married and had been in Canada an average of four years (range: one to eight years). The vast majority had taken ESL training courses upon arrival in Canada but none of the women identified themselves as being fluent in spoken English. As well, none of these women worked in the past year. Four of the women had completed high school, while the other two women had completed a university degree. When asked to rate their ability to financially make ends meet, based on their household income on a scale of one to six (one being "without any difficulty most months," and six being "we are not able to pay for most necessities many months"), the average rating was three, with two women describing their financial situation as a five and six.

A data analysis procedure based on hermeneutic phenomenological principles (Turner[3]) revealed four key findings known as *horizons of understanding*: Embracing a New Life, Realizing the Importance of a Strong Support Network, A Period of Learning, and Ongoing Challenges.

EMBRACING A NEW LIFE

For these women, the experience of being in a new country involved trying new things, embracing new customs, and even letting go of certain traditions. If they had been living in Sri Lanka, their families would have arranged many special rituals and practices to ensure their safe recovery from childbirth, protect the mother and infant from future problems (Dennis et al. 498), and acknowledge the woman's new role—that of mother. Examples of such practices include a three- to five-week long period of rest, prescribed practices for infant care and feeding, traditional means of ensuring a hygienic and warm environment for the mother and child, dietary restrictions for the mother, and organized support from close family members (Dennis et al. 488). In the absence of their extended family, these new mothers were introduced to formal government sponsored social and health care support services for women during the pregnancy and postpartum period, including in-home visits from public health nurses, pre- and post-natal classes, and access to a public health hotline with a Tamil translator. Such programs were new to the women in this study, and while useful for some new mothers, they lacked cultural relevancy and were regarded with mistrust by some mothers.

For some women, these services were a welcome source of support. For example, each woman was informed of the service of having an in-home visit from the public health nurse through their health care provider if they were in need of someone to show them aspects of care giving for their new baby. This is seen in Priya's testimony, "*That [public health] nurse helped me with feeding and bathing the child. At that time I had a stitch. When I would walk I would bleed so it was very helpful to have her.*" All but one of the participants received in-home visits by a nurse to help with breastfeeding, bathing, and other infant care-related issues. Two of the participants also attended pre-natal classes and had sought such services on their own. Tamil translators were available to assist them at these classes. One woman commented on the usefulness and value of the program, "[They were] *very useful … they helped me because there they taught us how to feed and take care of the baby*" (Lalita).

However, not all women availed of these services. Both Deepa and Lalita expressed the concern that many Tamil new mothers here in Canada do not make use of the services provided for new mothers. As Deepa explains:

I think the reason behind this is that these women don't seem to trust such services, since these are Canadian methods. I think they feel that performing such activities as bathing the baby and feeding the baby according to the norms of Canadians may prevent them from undertaking a more traditionally Tamil cultural upbringing.

This finding is consistent with research that has shown that the rates of utilization of pre- and postnatal care among immigrant women are lower than those of non-immigrant women (Landy et al 7). This finding is also supported by research showing that women who are at a socio-economic disadvantage (including immigrant women) may hold different expectations of pre- and postnatal education compared to women with more favourable economic situations, and in turn, are likely to express reluctance to go to pre- and postnatal classes (Comino and Harris 98). Other barriers of note to pre- and postnatal education among immigrant women include language barriers, difficulties with access to transportation to attend such classes, as well as a sense of unfamiliarity with the Canadian health care system, the latter of which is believed to weaken a newcomer's ability to properly access and use these services (Teng et al. 98-99).

REALIZING THE IMPORTANCE OF A STRONG SUPPORT NETWORK

All of the women in this study grew up in close-knit communities in Sri Lanka in which they were surrounded by their extended family. These communities were comprised of entire families living near one another but in separate houses. Several women expressed feelings of homesickness, of missing their parents, while they were adjusting to life in Canada "*I was missing my parents. Back home, all the relatives are there. When they're there, you don't realize it, only when you come here, you miss them*" (Lalita).

Living apart from their mother, however, was the most unbearable aspect of living in Canada, and appears to be the most common thread 'woven' through each woman's experience. The traditional Tamil family structure is patriarchal with men identified as the head of the household (Hyman et al. 146). However, women are the central figures when it comes to the birth of a child, with the new mother's own mother serving as the principal source of support (S. Meiyappan, Sr., personal communication, July 4th, 2010). For these women, in addition to providing help and advice in caring for a newborn, their mothers also represented a bearer of their Tamil culture—that is, someone who spoke in their language and knew the traditional customs that could be passed down to their daughters. This in turn could have made these women feel more confident in their new roles as mothers and less unsure as they negotiated the settlement process. All of the women in this study, however, were separated from their mothers during the migration and resettlement process, as well as for part or all of the pregnancy, delivery of their first child, and the post-partum period. The women universally expressed feeling sad and forlorn because of this separation "[the first] *six months, I was sad. Missing my mother...my father passed away. My mother looked after me* [while I grew up] " (Madhuri)

Another participant, Gaya, had arrived in Canada before her husband did. She did not have any advice for Tamil women who have already migrated to Canada, but did offer some additional thoughts for women who are still in Sri Lanka and have plans to migrate to Canada: "*I don't want anyone to go through what I went through. You should only come to Canada if your mother can come with you.*" By this, she is referring to her belief that a woman's mother plays an important role in guiding her through many stages in life, including giving birth to and caring for a baby. She went on to say:

> *The husband should also be here before you. If you have someone here, like an immediate family member, before you come, then it is okay. Even if you have an [older sister] or aunty, it is better. But not like me, like I came by myself, I do not like that.*

The women's mothers appeared to be their first line of support when it came to advice on such common but new events as putting a newborn to sleep and how to perform certain traditionally Tamil rituals such as massaging the baby's face and limbs with oil. The participants learned about such things from their mothers mainly by phone, and in one case, during conference calls with a third family member in another country. One woman also used Skype as a means of communicating with her family in Sri Lanka.

Even the two women in this study who used support services such as parenting classes for women during the pre- and postnatal periods in Toronto, noted they felt isolated and alone during their first year in Canada, despite the presence of their husbands. For instance, Deepa was the only woman who had attended post-natal classes (in addition to pre-natal classes), yet she still told us the following:

> *The first 45 days after the baby was born were very hard for me and my husband. I felt like crying because I realized that we both had so many family members back home, but we were here by ourselves. I missed support from my mother, aunts, and female cousins the most because if I was back home and had given birth there, they would have given me their undivided attention for those first one to two months.*

The lack of in-person support from friends and distant relatives appeared to be another key reason. One woman expressed how difficult it was to raise her first child with minimal support because all of her relatives were back home in Sri Lanka and she did not have any female friends here in Canada at the time "*Here I only know my husband's friends. I do not know of any females. Therefore there is no one to help*" (Priya).

The women in this study also described feeling reticent to ask for help from other Tamil women or families in Toronto. This is in keeping with the cultural notion of not wanting to impose on others, as exemplified by one of the participants who arrived in Canada eight months pregnant, before her husband joined her. She stated: "*I can't ask other people to come with me* [to the hospital]" (Gaya). Another woman did not want to overburden distant relatives living in the area "[My distant relative] *lives far, in another city, and she goes to work...* (Lalita). She went on to describe how this relative had organized a Tamil ceremony known as a *valaikappu* (similar to the Western baby shower), for Lalita. The *valaikappu* involves singing devotional songs and presenting the mother-to-be with new sets of bangles (bracelets). This event helped Lalita to feel a bit happier to be here because she was engaged in a ritual that was familiar and made her feel connected to other Tamil women. However, the women who attended were not close relatives as they would have been if the event were held back home, and while some of them came to visit Lalita shortly after the baby was born, there was no further contact beyond that time.

A PERIOD OF LEARNING

New motherhood in a new country is a period of deep learning. The women in this study spoke of how they felt unprepared to become mothers because they lacked the support and guidance of their mothers and extended family and community they had relied on in Sri Lanka. Without a ready source of guidance while adjusting to the new role of mother, the women in this study were faced with the prospect of having to learn about this on their own. "[The] *first time I gave baby a bath, I was scared to hold her head, the way the nurse had trained me...when I was by myself, I was scared,*" said Gaya. Another woman explained that she did not know how to even pick up her baby and learned through trial and error.

In addition to moments of fear and apprehension about learning to care for a child in the first few months after giving birth, two participants noted some positive aspects of becoming mothers for the first-time in a new country and expressed feelings of confidence, knowledge, and optimism after about six months after delivery. One woman also explained that giving birth to a baby in Canada helped her gain more experience than she would have "back home."

> *If I had given birth to the baby back home, I wouldn't have had all this experience—I wouldn't have this knowledge about how to look after a child because, back home, other than giving birth to the child, and breastfeeding it, all the other duties, like taking the child out and giving it a bath, would have been done by my mother, or my aunt, my cousins. Before, I was afraid to give the child a bath because I've never had to do it before. But now I can do it because I've learned how to, so I feel confident.* (Deepa)

These two women's sentiments were a deviant case, compared to the other women in this study. They both informed us that they are aware of this unique quality, as they both understand that a lot of Tamil women in the same situation do not hold these same attitudes towards embracing the ways of the new country and trying new things. They enjoyed their newfound autonomy and not having to share their mothering experience with their family. Deepa's philosophy in life was along the lines of: "*In life, if someone shoves you into the ocean, you have to learn how to swim.*" That is, no matter what situation she finds herself in, she would make the best of it. She went on to say that "*just because I am here without any family, I don't want to waste all my time crying over the loneliness; I want to do something to counter that.*"

Both women cited parenting classes as among the most memorable and important parts of their first year of becoming new mothers in a new country, as these helped ward off the sad and lonely feelings that came about from staying at home alone with the child, and they both learned a lot about taking care of a child. As Deepa commented, she considered these to be the most memorable and important parts of becoming a new mother,

> *instead of feeling tension from staying at home and feeling lonely, by going to these classes, not only would I be learning something about the child, but I would also be in a social setting, learning English. My English has improved because of that....* (Deepa)

After the baby is born, Deepa recommended that new mothers should also attend post-natal classes, or other programs for new mothers so that they can meet fellow new mothers for friendship, support, and advice. She said that it was here that she was able to talk to other women about educational items for her child, who in turn, advised her about their own ideas for raising a child: "*Now I can look at what other people are doing and I can also get those ideas and create my own. So it's pretty stimulating for my child, to not look at the same thing.*"

ONGOING CHALLENGES

For other women in the study, part of learning to raise a child was discovering traditions that Tamil mothers, regardless of where they live, try to follow. This also meant raising their children in a traditional fashion and ensuring that the children do not forget where their parents came from through bringing them up in the same way that the women themselves were raised in Sri Lanka. This was not, however, without its difficulties. For instance, visiting the temple was an almost daily ritual for several of the women in this study, when they lived in Sri Lanka. One participant, Gaya was unable to find a temple that she could go to regularly, for a long time after she first came here. When she finally did find one, she did not know how to go by herself.

Another woman expressed worry and concern over raising her child in an environment that was still foreign to her:

> *I'm kind of scared of raising a baby girl in a country like [this]. It's easier in Sri Lanka because you have all your family members and everyone can keep [an eye on her].... There was one time that I looked out the balcony because there I heard a lot of noise, and I saw two Tamil boys and one Tamil girl smoking cigarettes and being rowdy ... that's not the environment I was born and raised in. Everything is new here....* (Lalita)

Seeing Tamil children acting that way, which she felt was rowdier and less appropriate than the way Tamil children acted back home in Sri Lanka made her uneasy because this was a very different environment than the one she knew growing up. She felt that she did not know how to handle this situation because it was completely different from what she was used to back home. When she was growing up, her parents wanted to make sure that she was deeply embedded in her culture. Lalita feels that she does not want to lose her culture, including how parents raise their children, now that she lives in Toronto. Not only did this woman feel afraid of exposing her child to "bad" influences, but she also admitted that she wants to ensure the child does not forget where her parents came from: "*We don't want to lose our culture.*"

As well, while many of the women learned about traditional Tamil rituals that are normally done before and after a child is born through speaking with their own mothers over the phone, it was not always possible to carry these out. This was mainly due to the fact that most of the time no one was present to help them in performing these rituals, including preparing food in a certain traditional way, giving the baby an oil bath, and massage. Another important Tamil ritual that is performed about one month after a baby is born is the first haircut. One participant, Priya, told us that in the region where she is from in Sri Lanka, there are people (usually Hindu priests) who are specialized in cutting a baby's hair for the first time. She described her situation: "*I was not able to find anyone like that. As well, her son was born in the fall season so she was afraid that by cutting his hair bald, he might catch a cold.*"

All of these women had been enrolled in ESL classes upon arrival in Canada, with three women attending classes up to their ninth month of pregnancy. After giving birth, none of the women returned to these classes since they became busy with taking care of their child at home. While they were, for the most part, not completely satisfied in their level of English-speaking abilities, they did their best in communicating with the non-Tamil doctors, nurses, and other health care workers during the time of labour and delivery, and after having the baby. However, as Madhuri explained, the general sentiment at that time for all women (and continues to be) was:

If I was fluent in English, I think I would have had a better experience of becoming a mother. I would have felt more independent and confident when I spoke to the doctors, and maybe even more comfortable with accessing services for new mothers, like post-natal classes.

Each participant stated that she still had much more to learn and practice with her new language. Priya felt that being able to communicate with health care workers (such as hospital staff) and other women in Tamil would have made her experience of becoming a new mother a lot less difficult because she would have been able to communicate her needs and concerns more directly without having to rely on her husband or worse, remain silent.

CONCLUSION

The experience of first-time motherhood as a Tamil immigrant or refugee woman is marked by the intersection of two significant, transitional events in these women's lives: migration and motherhood. The challenge for the new mothers in our study was learning how to raise a child in a way that retained their cultural values while living in a new country, and also learning how to become an independent and confident mother. They also had to try and embrace a new life that included new experiences such as accepting help from formal social and health care support services during the pregnancy and postpartum period, in the absence of a familial support network. Having a better understanding of the way in which immigrant or refugee women experience first-time motherhood and the meanings they ascribe to the experience is one step towards ensuring that the health and social service providers who work with these women will respond effectively and appropriately to these women's needs and concerns.

Moreover, this study did not focus on a psychiatric diagnosis, or a problem known to affect a significant proportion of new mothers, namely postpartum depression (PPD), a problem that affects ten to fifteen percent of Western women (O'Hara and Swain 45). It is possible that PPD is not a culturally relevant concept to Tamil women and that their distress, albeit a reality, is simply expressed in terms that are different than their Canadian-born counterparts who have become mothers for the first-time and do have a clear psychiatric diagnosis of PPD. That is, PPD may need to be examined more closely since there are many reasons why women may seem "depressed" after having a baby—especially newcomer women. Therefore, through this study we hope to provide health care and service providers with more culturally and experientially based views of difficulties faced by new Tamil mothers than the clinical label of "postpartum depression." It is hoped that this dissemination of our work may influence practice guidelines as well as treatment and counselling procedures now in place for Tamil women, resulting in both more patient-centred and culturally informed care.

As well as informing social service providers, through this study, we also sought to raise awareness in the Tamil community about potentially un- or under met needs and experiences of Tamil immigrant or refugee women who are first-time mothers. This study may provide an opportunity for the voices of the participants and women like them to be heard by decision-makers and influential persons in the Tamil community. This is important for the participants in our study, as they wanted to help other newcomer Tamil women who are first-time mothers. If this awareness is raised, new Tamil mothers will get the help they need from their community as well.

While this study has enhanced our understanding of the experience of becoming a first-time mother for Tamil immigrant or refugee woman, more research is needed to ensure that the mental health care needs of these women are addressed.

The authors would like to thank the small, but hardworking, group of volunteer bilingual fieldworkers who provided tremendous support in the form of translation, interpretation, and overall passion for this project. We would also like to extend our thanks to the individuals from settlement agencies that comprised our community advisory group: Ms. Sudharshana Coomarasamy, Women's Health Centre, St. Joseph's Health Centre (Toronto); Ms. Shyamala Shanmuganathan, Polycultural Immigrant and Community Services; and Ms. Sivajini Jegatheeswaran, St. James Town Health Centre, St. Michael's Hospital. Finally, we are immensely grateful to the women who participated in our study and welcomed us into their homes to share their experiences of becoming new mothers in a new country.

ENDNOTES

[1] For the purposes of this paper, immigrants or refugees who have arrived in Canada within the last five to ten years will be identified as "newcomers."
[2] Note that this is fairly different from thematic analysis in which codes or labels are applied to significant segments of transcripts in order to reduce data to categories and themes (Creswell). Thematic analysis is not in line with the cyclical nature of engagement with the data and movement towards a greater understanding through entering the hermeneutic circle that is found in hermeneutic phenomenology. Researchers carrying out a hermeneutic phenomenological study describe their findings as *horizons of understanding*, rather than labelling them as themes.
[3] As Gadamer himself did not explicate specific research steps to be followed, this study used the data analysis procedures set forth by Turner, who incorporated Gadamer's philosophical underpinnings into her study of hope seen through the eyes of Australian youth.

WORKS CITED

Ahmed, Amal, Donna Stewart, Lily Teng, Olive Wahoush and Anita Gagnon. "Experiences of Immigrant New Mothers with Symptoms of Depression." *Archives of Women's Mental Health* 11 (2008): 295-303. Print.

Comino, Elizabeth J. and Elizabeth Harris. "Maternal and Infant Services: Examination of Access in a Culturally Diverse Community." *Journal of Paediatric Child Health* 39 (2003): 95-99. Print.

Creswell, John. *Qualitative Inquiry and Research Design: Choosing Among Five Approaches.* 2nd ed. Thousand Oaks, California: Sage Publications, Inc., 2006. Print.

Dennis, Cindy-Lee, et al. "Traditional Postpartum Practices and Rituals: A Qualitative Systematic Review." *Women's Health* 3.4 (2007): 487-502. Print.

Gadamer, Hans-Georg. *Truth and Method.* 1972. 2nd rev. ed. Trans. Joel Weinsheimer and Donald G. Marshall. New York: Continuum, 1989. Print.

Guruge, Sepali and Enid Collins, eds. *Working with Immigrant Women: Issues and Strategies for Mental Health Professionals.* Toronto: Centre for Addiction and Mental Health, 2008. Print.

Hilton, B. Ann, et al. "The Desi Ways: Traditional Health Practices of South Asian Women in Canada." *Health Care for Women International* 22.6 (2001): 553-67. Print.

Hyman, Ilene, et al. "Perceptions of and Responses to Woman Abuse Among Tamil Women in Toronto." *Canadian Woman Studies/les cahiers de la femme* 25.1,2 (2006): 145-50. Print.

Koch, Tina. "Interpretive approaches in nursing research: The influence of Husserl and Heidegger." *Journal of Advanced Nursing* 21 (1995): 827-836. Print.

Landy, Christine Kurtz, Wendy Sword and Donna Ciliska. "Urban Women's Socioeconomic Status, Health Service Needs and Utilization in the Four Weeks After Postpartum Hospital Discharge: Findings of a Canadian Cross-Sectional Survey." *BMC Health Services Research* 8 (2008): 1-9. Print.

Liamputtong, Pranee and Charin Naksook. "Life as Mothers in a New Land: The Experience of Motherhood Among Thai Women in Australia." *Health Care for Women International* 24.7 (2003): 650-668. Print.

Morrow, Marina, Jules E. Smith, Yuan Lai, and Suman Jaswal. "Shifting Landscapes: Immigrant Women and Postpartum Depression." *Health Care for Women International* 29.6 (2008): 593-617.

O'Hara, Michael W. and Annette M. Swain. "Rates and Risk of Postpartum Depression—A Meta-Analysis." *International Review of Psychiatry* 8.1 (1996): 37-54. Print.

Stewart, Donna E., et al. "Postpartum Depression Symptoms in Newcomers." *Canadian Journal of Psychiatry* 53.2 (2008): 121-24. Print.

Teng, Lilly, Emma Robertson Blackmore and Donna E. Stewart. "Health-care Worker's Perceptions of Barriers to Care by Immigrant Women with Postpartum Depression: An Exploratory Qualitative Study." *Archives of Women's Mental Health* 10 (2007): 93-101. Print.

Turner, de Sales. "Horizons Revealed: From Methodology to Method." *International Journal of Qualitative Methods* 2.1 (2003): 1-32. Print.

Wilcke, Margaretha M. "Hermeneutic Phenomenology as a Research Method in Social Work." *Currents: New Scholarship in the Human Services* 1.1 (2002): 1-10. Print.

Zelkowitz, Phyllis, et al. "Stability and Change in Depressive Symptoms from Pregnancy to Two Months Postpartum in Childbearing Immigrant Women." *Archives of Women's Mental Health* 11 (2008): 1-11. Print.

South Asian Mothers with Special Needs Children

SATWINDER KAUR BAINS

S OUTH ASIAN MOTHERS of differently abled children face numerous barriers accessing culturally relevant support and services for their children, and themselves. This chapter outlines a study of care-giving mothers in the small rural town of Abbotsford, British Colombia. This work was based on the premise that "disability" has an enormous stigma attached to it for South Asian families, due to the particular socio-cultural and historical frame of reference attached to disability. In this context, mothers may be blamed for the disability, find limited support from family and the wider community, and be weary of going outside the South Asian community for help. Through this chapter I will offer insight on how South Asian mothers parenting a child with a disability navigate the challenges they experience.

The impetus for this study was the growing recognition in the social services sector that services should meet the needs of ethnically diverse community groups and individuals. South Asian families were targeted for this study because of the growing South Asian population in the Abbotsford area. People of South Asian heritage now make up approximately 18 percent of the total population, an increase of seven percent in five years. Of the 32,195 visible minorities identified in the 2006 census, 72.5 percent (23,355) classified themselves as South Asians, making it the top ethnic ancestry after European. The most commonly spoken language in the home after English is Punjabi at 39.3 percent. The number of immigrants from India to Abbotsford has risen by 20 percent over the last five years and all indications are that the local area will continue to be attractive to the South Asian community in the foreseeable future as a destination for settlement (Census Canada).

BACKGROUND AND RELEVANCY OF STUDY

It is important to understand the power relations and cultural mores of South Asian family systems and the role of women as mothers and care-givers of children with disabilities (Mullender et al.). Traditionally, power and parenting are organized hierarchically in South Asian families, with men generally having more power than women, mothers parenting more actively than fathers, and elders having more power than youth (Deepak). The community often, but not always, takes the place of kin; for example when family supports are lost through migration (Shirwadkar). Given the historically key role of extended family members and the community in family functioning, it is especially important to assess the degree of isolation and/or support available to immigrant South Asian mothers raising children with disabilities (Maiter, Alaggia and Trocmé).

The concept of acculturation suggests a one-sided adaptation to the host culture when in fact the process is much more complex. Indeed, Anne Deepak proposes to replace acculturation with the broader construct of the immigration process as "...a set of shifting and conflicting demands, expectations and possibilities centered on gender, power, culture and sexuality coming from the ideologies, structural conditions, and cultural and social norms of the home and host countries" (590). Within this framework mothering is challenged by the primary and intrinsic need to provide care to children.

There is an assumption that people from minority ethnic groups have large and supportive extended family networks and therefore do not need or want the support of social services (Atkins and Rolling). However, research indicates that this is not always the case, and that the nature and extent of supports vary greatly (Hatton et al. 2002; Thoburn, Chand and Proctor; Atkin and Rollings).

Chris Hatton et al. (2002) investigated the experiences of 136 South Asian families with a child with severe disabilities in the United Kingdom and found that there are many reasons why South Asian parents lacked support from their extended families. There are practical issues such as family members being too busy to help. Parents reported that extended family members sometimes were not interested in the child, did not know that their family members needed help and sometimes held cultural views on disabilities that prohibited interaction. These views were based on ideas about getting help from traditional healers, the possibility of a "cure" and notions of disability creating "difference" (Hatton et al. 2002).

Since South Asian mothers of children with disabilities report less extended family or friends support, it is not surprising that they would want support from external services. However, they often do not access formal support for various reasons such as: lack of awareness of services that are available; inefficiency of services; and cultural barriers (Baxter et al.; Hatton et al. 1998, 2002; Chamba et al.; Mir et al.). A lack of parental awareness has also been linked to relatively low access to family support services such as respite care and family support groups. As well, there is also some evidence that services targeting South Asian families with lower household incomes are inefficient with families receiving fewer services (Hatton et al. 1998). Finally, South Asian families have identified culturally inappropriate and inadequate services and racism as significant barriers to the uptake and continued use of services (Shah 1995, 2006; Hatton et al. 2004). The need for ethnically integrated services that routinely met their child's language, cultural and religious needs were consistently reported as necessary areas of improvement (Hatton).

As scholars show, as the primary caregivers, South Asian mothers experience the most strain due to the lack of adequate support and services for their children. In a study in the UK, 54 South Asian mothers caring for children with disabilities were interviewed regarding family circumstances, service supports and levels of stress (Hatton et al, 1998). The study found that South Asian mothers of a child with a disability were frequently becoming mentally and physically stressed resulting in a higher number of family doctor and hospital visits for their own health needs and elevated levels of distress signalling mental health problems. The two main factors that most contributed to this breakdown were lower household incomes and caring for more than one child with a disability (Hatton et al. 1998). Mothers reported drop-in centres, quality home support services and gender-specific services as being potentially valuable resources for improving family life (Hatton).

Understanding and acceptance of their child's disability by both parents is a crucial influence on the support process. South Asian families caring for children with disabilities and mothers in particular need extensive support. The formal and informal support provided to South Asian mothers does not meet their needs adequately. For many South Asian families who have a child with severe disabilities, a pattern of real disadvantages emerges as household incomes of families are low, unemployment is high and housing is unsuitable for the needs of the family (particularly in terms of lack of space and safety issues) (Shah 2006; Ahmad and Atkin; Modood et al.; Nazroo 1997, 1998; Shah 2006). Since many South Asian mothers who care for a child with severe disabilities have difficulty accessing information and resources for their child and are less recognized as needing services by service professionals and general society, they are often in isolation.

METHOD

It is within the context of a significant population base that a study of South Asian families who live in the Abbotsford area and have one or more children with disabilities, was undertaken in 2009. Focus group interviews were used as part of a qualitative research method (Kreuger; Morgan). Focus groups provide an interactive process for individuals to share information, and to respond to each other in a peer focused forum. The open-ended questions used for the study allowed for extensive discussion, providing a space for participants to describe their perceived needs at this particular point in time (Yegidis, Weinbach and Meyers). Focus groups allowed the individual and family experiences of the mothers (e.g., experiences, actions, reactions, and demands) to be brought into a clearer focus and to the attention of the researcher. This was also a space where participants could make sense of the points where individual experiences and institutional services intersected. In a reflective process, participants and the researcher could make a connection between peoples' experiences of social services and their lives (Evans).

Recruitment to the focus groups was done through bilingual (English and Punjabi) posters at the social service agency that mothers visited with their children, utilizing convenience sampling through word of mouth, and the snowball method. Twenty South Asian mothers took part in three focus groups at the social service agency. Each focus group lasted for two hours and consisted of six to seven mothers. All of the women had oral English language skills. However, their Punjabi oral skills were much greater, so the focus groups were mostly conducted in Punjabi. Their experiences in Canada were diverse although their own cultural heritage was similar. Their experiences capture a particular perspective of South Asian mothers who are relationally living with a disability through their children. All the mothers are in contact with a social service agency assessing some services for their children.

FINDINGS

The findings from the focus groups indicate that there were a number of areas of stress and concern for the mothers as they sought services for their children. These included: cultural stigma towards disability, insularity of the South Asian community, their own limited understanding of the political and economic issues surrounding provision of disability services, lack of family support, isolation and apathy. However, despite these obstacles some of the mothers were also motivated to provide support for each other and find avenues for voicing their needs/concerns, while advocating for other mothers who may have had no other advocacy avenues.

The focus groups invariably started with the "moment of truth" when mothers found out that their child had a disability—whether it was at birth, shortly after or much later. Whenever it was, regardless of the time-frame, their initial reaction was of dismay and shock, followed closely by having to deal with interference of others' perceptions of disability. Mothers concurred when Jasbir (pseudonyms are used for mothers in this study) said, "I was made to feel as if I had somehow produced the disability." There was a pervasive sentiment/accusation from family members and friends that something had gone wrong in the pregnancy and that the mother was responsible. This indicated to the mothers very clearly that much needs to be done to educate family and community about the causes and reasons a child has a disability. The blaming, shaming and naming was something mothers felt ill-equipped to deal with as they themselves were unaware of the issue at hand.

When these mothers did reach out for support, it was initially from within their network of family and friends. As Harwant stated, "I have to rely on key people in the immediate family for information, because first my family is the one I ask and I don't look outside until much later." This initial help is limited by the family members' own attitudes towards disability, and a lack of awareness of services and support. In this initial crucial stage much valuable time was lost, to the detriment of the child's well-being. Part of the reason for the lack of awareness is the limited interaction with mainstream social service agencies (which provide a bulk of services) in the daily lives of the participants. This limits their access to information, especially if no effort is made by service-providing agencies to reach out to ethno-racial communities in a culturally relevant manner. Harpal echoed group sentiments when she wondered, "Do agencies think no disabilities occur in the South Asian population?" Amanjot said:

> I felt so much confusion about services, especially since I am a new immigrant and I do not have fluency in English. I didn't know who offers what, what does the program mean, what is the referral process, what is the requirement to join / receive services, is it free, does it have a child care component, etc. At home (in India) we did not have these kinds of services.

The mothers expressed passivity to some degree about the quality and extent of services that they currently receive. Further probing brought forth answers about their needs that were not being met on a comprehensive scale. Also, when asked about services for their children as they become young adults, there were limited projections about future needs (e.g. needs of children with disabilities transitioning to adulthood). Darshan articulated that, "I usually ask the bilingual service provider about what I should do; she usually has all the answers. How would I know?" It appears the mothers have not explored their own needs in the area of assessment of future needs for their children.

The mothers in this study felt that as close-knit as the South Asian community is, it is also very exclusionary when a mental illness, disability or other social ill is present in the home. As a result, the mothers explained that the social isolation for mothers who have a child with disabilities, is only relieved when they access services and meet other mothers in similar situations. The stress of stigmatization was keenly felt by the mothers, although they also expressed an empowerment of sorts as they considered themselves "lucky" to be receiving services. At various times they discussed how they have felt the sting of rejection, ignorance or blame, but they unequivocally claimed that the child was their first priority and they would do anything to ensure that they protected him or her.

The mothers were also mostly resigned to the fact that although over time their extended family members became largely supportive of them, they still felt isolated due to the burden faced as primary care givers. As well, it was felt that the mothers' responsibilities in the home did not diminish with the increased level of care-giving required for the disabled child. Their identity as South Asian wives and mothers kept them tied to cultural traditions and sometimes a decrease in status was apparent when a disabled child was born. They had very few places to share their needs or concerns. An often solitary tale of mothers caring for the needs of the disabled children emerged.

The mothers reported that fathers took a more passive role in inquiry and left it up to the primary caregiver (usually the mother) to assess the child's progress and to further question difficulties and seek assistance. The mothers did not show a critical response to the lack of father involvement; they had limited or no expectations of involvement by their partner. As Harjinder stated, "He is so busy with his work that he gives little time to the care and needs of our child." Mothers told of their days and nights taken up in the care of their household duties and that their own needs were often ignored or put on hold in order to do what was necessary. Partner involvement was not an option and the mothers had resigned themselves to that fact. However, Navneet had a different experience with her spouse and told the group about her spouse's empathy and solidarity to their situation. "Really?" the other mothers asked, "What does he do, how does he help?" Navneet described, "He is always asking me what he can do, telling me to rest when he is around and he helps around the house with all the chores." However, usually, the mothers agreed that their own needs took a secondary position to all the other members of the family in the household.

However, now that these mothers knew about the services that they are accessing, they are also thinking about how to help other mothers in similar situations. "Even if my experience has not been the best in terms of access, I feel in a stronger and better position to advocate for other mothers, children and their families" Harpal stated. The form and type of advocacy that they envisioned was not articulated clearly, however, initial forms of assistance such as being available to meet with new mothers needing help, on the phone or in person was suggested by the mothers, reflecting upon personal growth and agency. The mothers felt that support groups for South Asian mothers would be beneficial so that they could share with others experiencing the same things as them. "How should we get heard? Whom do we speak to?" Balwinder asked.

In the focus group they offered to help each other and new mothers in the future. Opportunities to give "voice" to their experiences were recognized as important.

CONCLUSION

It is abundantly apparent from this study that South Asian mothers who are currently accessing services for their children with a disability have difficulties—arising from their specific cultural context—that can impact service provision. Preliminary findings suggest that prevention and on-going programs and services that are bilingual, bi-cultural and culturally relevant are needed to meet the unique needs of South Asian mothers. Empirical evidence is needed to document the nature of services and their effectiveness in the various disability domains to assess how South Asian families can effectively access information and utilize services to meet the needs of their children with a disability.

As a first step we have established that South Asian mothers are the primary care givers of children with disabilities and shoulder a large burden to ensure that their children receive the services they require. However, the support for their own needs (e.g. to be advocates or to give "voice" to their experiences) is lacking and these mechanisms need to be studied and reported. Stepping outside their traditional norms and offering active support to each other in gendered spaces also requires perseverance on the part of South Asian mothers. As this study showed, social service agencies can serve as nodal points for the mothers to meet, discuss and plan how to support each other through the stresses they experience.

WORKS CITED

Ahmad, Waqar I. U. and Karl Atkin. *"Race" and Community Care.* Buckingham: Open University Press, 1996. Print.

Atkin, Karl and Janet Rollings. "Looking After Their Own? Family Care-giving Among Asian and Afro-Caribbean Communities." *"Race" and Community Care.* Eds. W. I. U. Ahmad and K. Atkin. Buckingham: Open University Press, 1996. 73-86. Print.

Baxter, Carol, Kamaljit Poonia, Linda Ward, Zenobia Nadirshaw and Angela Martin. *Double Discrimination: Issues and Services for People with Learning Difficulties from Black and Minority Ethnic Commu-*

nities. London: King's Fund Centre, 1990. Print.

Chamba, Rampaul, Waqar Ahmad, Michael Hirst, Dot Lawton and Bryony Beresford. *On The Edge: Minority Ethnic Families Caring For A Severely Disabled Child.* Bristol: The Policy Press, 1999. Print.

Census Canada. *Canada's Ethnocultural Mosaic: 2006 Census National Picture.* Ottawa: Government Press, 2006. Print.

Deepak, Anne C. "Parenting and the Process of Migration: Possibilities Within South Asian Families." *Child Welfare.* 84.5 (2005): 585-606. Accessed 21 June 2009. Web.

Evans, Mary. "Reading Lives: How the Personal Might Be Social." *Sociology* 27.1 (1993): 5-13. Print.

Hatton, Chris. *Supporting South Asian Families with a Child with Severe Disabilities.* Philadelphia: Jessica Kingsley Publishers, 2004. Print.

Hatton, Chris, Sabiha Azmi, Amanda Caine and Eric Emerson. "Informal Carers of Adolescents and Adults with Learning Difficulties from the South Asian Communities: Family Circumstances, Service Support and Carer Stress." *British Journal of Social Work* 28.6 (1998): 821-837. Print.

Hatton, Chris, Yasmeen Akram, Janet Robertson, Robina Shah and Eric Robertson. "The Disclosure Process and its Impact on South Asian Families with a Child with Severe Intellectual Disabilities." *Journal of Applied Research in Intellectual Disabilities* 16.3 (2003): 177. Print.

Hatton, Chris, Yasmeen Akram, Robina Shah, Janet Robertson and Eric Emerson. *Supporting South Asian Families with a Child with Severe Disabilities: A Report to the Department of Health.* Lancaster: Institute for Health Research, Lancaster University, 2002. Print.

Kreuger, Richard A. *Focus Groups: a Practical Guide for Applied Research.* London: Sage, 1988. Print.

Maiter, Sarah, Ramona Alaggia and Nico Trocmé. "Perceptions of Child Maltreatment from the Indian Subcontinent: Challenging Myths About Culturally Based Abusive Parenting Practices." *Child Maltreatment* 9.3 (2004): 309-324. Accessed 13 June 2009. Web.

Mir, Ghazala, Andrew Nocon, Ahmad Waqar and Lesley Jones. *Learning Difficulties and Ethnicity.* London: Department of Health, 2001. Print.

Morgan David L. *Focus Groups as Qualitative Research.* 2nd ed. London: Sage Publications, 1997. Print.

Modood, Tariq, Richard Berthoud, Jane Lakey, Jane Nazroo, Patten Smith, Satnam Virdee and Sharon Beishon. *Ethnic Minorities in Britain: Diversity and Disadvantage.* London: Policy Studies Institute, 1997. Print.

Mullender, Andrew, Gill Hague, Umme Imam, Liz Kelly, Ellen Malos and Linda Regan. "Barriers of Racism, Ethnicity and Culture." *Children's Perspectives on Domestic Violence*. Ed. A. Mullender et al. London: Sage, 2002. 132-155. Print.

Nazroo, James Y. *The Health of Britain's Ethnic Minorities*. London: Policy Studies Institute, 1997. Print.

Nazroo, James Y. *Ethnicity and Mental Health: Findings from a National Community Survey*. London: Policy Studies Institute, 1998. Print.

Shah Robina. *The Silent Minority: Children with Disabilities in Asian Families*. London: National Children's Bureau, 1995. Print.

Shah Robina. "Race, Ethnicity and Culture-Proving Intimate and Personal Care within a 'Person-Centred' Approach." *Intimate and Personal Care with People with Learning Disabilities*. Ed. S. Carnaby and P. Cambridge. London: Jessica Kingsley Publishers, 2006. 33-43. Print.

Shirwadkar, Swati. "Canadian Domestic Violence Policy and Indian Immigrant Women." *Violence Against Women* 10.8 (2004): 860-879. Accessed July 21 2009. Web.

Thoburn, June, Ashok Chand and Joanne Proctor. *Child Welfare Services for Minority and Ethnic Families*. London: Jessica Kingsley Publishers, 2005. Print.

Yegidis, Bonnie L., Robert W. Weinbach and Laura L. Meyers. *Research Methods for Social Workers*. 4th Ed. Toronto: Allyn and Bacon, 2006. Print.

Mothers and Warriors

SADIA ZAMAN

H E IS BORN by c-section, our second child. He is a big baby. He does not cry. My husband puts the baby's face to mine and we stare at each other for the first time. I cry because I am amazed, and because I am The Mother. Hours later the baby is in an incubator and I'm not sure why, something about loud breathing. Two years later I would be shocked when I see the video for the first time. Shocked to learn that this is the moment it had all started. The truth is, I could never remember when it all began.

He is three months old and has a cough that does not go away for two days. Our daughter had been such a healthy baby, so I do not worry until the night he refuses to nurse. The next morning we all walk to the clinic. The receptionist takes one look at the baby and asks the doctor to examine him immediately. We are stunned. The doctor gives me a mask with medication that will loosen the fluid in my son's lungs. I hold it so I can't see his tiny face. He does not cry. Slowly my tears fall and mix with the medication he inhales. I am The Mother, how could I let this happen?

We are sent to the hospital and admitted but have to stay in the emergency ward because there are no beds. The nurses explain that my son's lungs don't work the way they're supposed to. I hold a mask to my son's face every half hour, every hour, every two hours. Slowly he begins to nurse again. There is another Mother with a three-year-old who is also wearing a mask. I am humbled when I think of all the months, weeks, days, hours and seconds she must have endured this laboured breathing. Humbled because I know I do not have it in me to watch my child fight for breath. Twenty-four hours of it have almost broken me. But you see I do not yet know about The Warrior and what she looks like.

In the morning we are released, and I am so thrilled to go home. I desperately want to sleep. But within an hour the baby starts to throw up thick mucus. He begins to choke. We are back at the hospital. This time they send us to another hospital with an empty bed and a paediatrician who specializes in asthma. In the car I swallow the tears because I slowly begin to realize that I am now The Mother of a child who is not well. How will I protect him from bad air, the common cold, and other children?

He is hooked up to a monitor, a heart machine, and a cocktail of drugs that will bring down the inflammation in his airways. He is pale, tiny, and lifeless. Every time he takes a breath, he pulls in his stomach, ribs protruding, only to struggle for the next breath. I put my ear to his chest because I want to hear something, anything. His face scrunches up in preparation for a cry that I cannot hear. He has lost his voice. I want to scream.

And this is the moment; the very moment that I become The Warrior. I don the armour that all Mothers have, the one that protects us during years of sleep deprivation and fatigue. I borrow a shield from the eyes of a Mother in the emergency room. Her child has just been hit by a car. I carry a sword, the same one the Mother next door uses to fight the cancerous cells that attack her little girl's body.

The Warrior's determined battle plan prevents me from asking WHY? I am methodical, organized, focused. I nurse my son every hour for a minute or two until his lungs become too tired. We slowly work our way up to ten minutes. He avoids being fed through the IV. I monitor his oxygen level fanatically, and I sing until my voice is hoarse. The nurses do not have to wake me for night feedings; I do not sleep.

One day he puts on weight, only to lose it two days later. One day the doctor tells me he'll be just fine, another day I'm told he's not making progress. I call my boss to cancel our meeting to discuss my eventual return to work. I do not mind when best friends with young children do not call me. They tell me it is too painful. The Warrior does not hold it against them, for she carries the strongest shield.

The shield is coated with the laughter and exquisite chocolate my sister brings to the hospital. The armour strengthened by my brothers and sisters-in-law as they lend me one shoulder to lean on and carry our daughter on the other. The sword has been dipped in My Mother's haunting prayers, determined to bring Allah onside. My mother carries her own sword, wrapped in her hijab, the white scarf she started wearing the day of my father's funeral.

The Warrior's uniform is invisible to all except the baby's father. My battered husband tucks me in at the hospital every night, covers me with a blanket woven with intense devotion. For The Warrior knows it is much warmer than one stitched with mere love. He tells me a joke, then tucks our daughter into the narrow hospital bed with me. I put my ear on her back and hear the strong, steady rhythm of her breath.

The next day my daughter and I lie on a bench in the hospital grounds and stare at the sky. She asks me if her brother, the baby she's only known for three months, is going to heaven like her grandfather. No, The Warrior says with absolute certainty. The grandfather, my father, was killed in a car accident when I was seven months pregnant with the baby boy. No one knows, but the grandfather has come to the hospital every night and held The Warrior's hand. He has given his daughter not only his face, but also The Warrior's fierce determination. Besides, he has already checked to make sure Allah placed an angel on each of the grandson's shoulders. And for extra protection, he gave the baby his last breath the moment the semi-truck hit the car.

Nine days later, the baby and The Warrior leave the hospital. The following month the baby will formally be diagnosed with severe asthma. The Warrior will administer blue puffers, green puffers, brown puffers, and orange ones. She will become an expert at using the aerochamber and know all about beta agonists. There will be weekly visits to the clinic to monitor his breathing. But despite The Warrior's battle plan, there will be many more hospital visits over the next two years, and the baby boy will develop pneumonia at least five times. He will have his body forced into a plastic harness with his arms suspended over his head to have his chest x-rayed repeatedly. He will take countless doses of oral steroids; some will give him constant diarrhea. The blue puffers will raise the baby's heart rate erratically, and The Mother will be told that his bones may become weak from all the medication.

The Warrior takes turns with her husband holding the baby upright through endless nights. And when he has a cold she is ready for battle. She sweeps all dust from the baby's life and forbids stuffed animals.

The daughter no longer wants this baby brother. Or This Mother. She wants The Mother who jumps out of trees and falls to her knees. Not This Mother who shows up in her drawings with an upside-down smile and a purple heart. She is sure This Mother has forgotten how to cry. The baby brother has taken too much and The Mother has given him everything. When The Mother recoils from the pain of the accusation, it is The Warrior who faces the anger, head on.

When The Mother is sentimental about the baby outgrowing his baby face, his babble, his waddle, The Warrior gives away all baby clothes and makes a mental note of every month that passes. The older he gets, the stronger his airways. The Warrior also forces The Mother back to work when The Mother is convinced she cannot leave this child, ever.

The baby now a toddler, runs into a window ledge at full speed and cracks his forehead open. The Mother panics at the sight of skull, the lack of blood. But The Warrior only worries that the shock and pain will bring on an asthma attack. She must calm this toddler who has now learned to wail at the top of his lungs. On the way to the hospital, it is The Warrior who speaks in a clear, controlled voice. The Mother is asked to leave the room when they sew his forehead together. Nine stitches. The Warrior stays close enough to hear him cry. A nurse says mothers of asthmatics are unusually calm. But she does not know what is going on inside This Mother's head. Why did she not coddle this boy more, use the eyes in the back of her head? But The Warrior is adamant; she expects this child to do what all other children his age do. That is to demand everything, to laugh himself hoarse, and yes, to crash into window ledges and get hurt.

Over the next few months there will be many more hurts. But The Mother will get some unexpected help. Every once in a while, the daughter will run into the room breathless, to warn The Mother that her brother has started coughing. And sometimes, The Mother will notice that the daughter will cup her brother's head in her hands to sing to him when he has to take his puffers. The Warrior will still calm The Mother when there is a flu epidemic at the daughter's school, when The Mother is sure she can hear the baby wheezing from her office downtown, when the fear of SARS wakes her in a cold sweat.

Today the baby, now a little boy, turns three. He takes a deep breath, fills his lungs with air and blows out all three candles with a vengeance. The Mother watches as he shares the first bite of chocolate cake with the daughter. And later, after the loot bags have been handed out, and The Mother has put her ear on the little boy's chest to hear the steady sound of his breathing, I turn on the computer. Tonight The Warrior has stored her shield in the attic, put down the sword for the first time, and inspected the armour for cracks. She pretends not to notice the water dripping from her eyes, pretends not to wince every time my fingers hit the keyboard to write these words. The Mother smiles, laughs out loud. Welcome to Motherhood.

Mothering the South Asian Mother

Stories from Midwifery

MANAVI HANDA

I AM A BELIEVER in narrative. Storytelling is an old tradition in passing on women's herstory and a common pedagogical tool in midwifery education. While this is my story, it is not mine alone. It is instead, the story of the South Asian mothers who have come to me for their care.

I entered the midwifery program in 1999, five years after it had been legislated in Ontario—the first province to do so in Canada. Our current form of midwifery was born out of the women's health movement and as a result, generally began with a group of fairly privileged feminist white women, serving similarly privileged women (Bourgeault; Bourgeault, Benoit and Davis-Floyd; Nestel). I began my career as a young, idealistic feminist, hoping to become one of a handful of registered midwives of colour and serve marginalized women. It is this idealism that originally spurred me to do outreach to women of the South Asian community.

As a new midwife, realizing that there was very little knowledge about midwifery in the South Asian community, I started doing basic outreach. I began by leaving flyers at nearby mosques and community centers saying that I speak Hindi, Urdu and Punjabi (which was a bit of a stretch as my vocabulary in these languages is essentially equivalent to that of a ten year old). Over the past years I have done a fair amount of work with new South Asian immigrant women. As a child of South Asian immigrant parents, there are parts of the newcomer struggle that are very familiar to me. However, when I first started working with this community, I felt I was also witness to a new kind of struggle—one I was completely unfamiliar with and had never heard about in South Asian or political circles.

As a new midwife, working with South Asian newcomers, I started coming across more and more women from the sub-continent who were here in Canada through legitimate means but without any access to health insurance. It is the story of these women that I have chosen to tell. I can think of many women I have served over the years whose account I could share—Sarabjeet, Surinder, Fauzia, Fatima, Roopa, Soniya. They are all different women. They speak different languages, come from different regions of South Asia, have different religions, and different castes and classes. Arriving here, however, they are somewhat equalized into being the same—poor, brown, isolated, scared, and alone. They are strange women in a strange land—exotified or treated with curiosity at best—but more often, discriminated against or just invisible.

While I recognize their differences, I have chosen in this story to make them generic, in the same way that Canada and migration also blur them into sameness. While I know they are vastly different and I connected with each of them in different ways, here I have amalgamated them into one woman, and created an "archetype." I do this, not to further disempower immigrant women, but to draw on familiar threads in their collective experience. Forgive me the transgression, it was the best way I could give them a voice and tell their largely unknown story. Here I have chosen to tell the story of the typical South Asian woman I see in my care. I have chosen to call her Fatima.

FATIMA'S STORY

Soon after starting my midwifery practice, I get a phone call from a Pakistani woman in her last month of pregnancy. I arrange to have her meet me for an appointment. She comes to the clinic with her three young children, fully clad from head to toe in a black burqa—even her hands are covered with gloves. I don't quite have the words to express how out of place she looks in our practice waiting room, where we have almost solely served white Caucasian women.[1]

I take her into the office and start explaining the philosophy of midwifery care to her; the one-on-one care, continuity of care giver and philosophy of informed choice.[2] *She stops me mid-sentence and simply says, "Someone told me that you would take care of me and it would be free, is that true?" That, essentially, is the bottom line; she is not interested in my feminist ideology. I explain that yes, midwives in Ontario are funded to*

care for all residents of the province, regardless of immigration status.[3]
*With relief, she silently starts weeping and finally lifts her head scarf so I
can see her face—she smiles with extreme gratitude. "Ma'Shallah, I'm so
glad I found you, I didn't know what I was going to do. When we came
here, I was told in Canada all health care is free. We spent years waiting
for our immigration papers and spent all of our savings to come here.
We were so happy that this child would be born in Canada. Then when
I landed, every doctor I went to told me I wouldn't have free health care
for three months and they wanted to take thousands of dollars to look
after me. They wouldn't even see me without taking money first. I even
thought of going back home to have my baby, but they said I couldn't
fly because my due date is so close."*

Her story is the same as thousands of immigrant women who come
to Toronto each year. It often takes years to get approval for landed
immigration status—for those lucky enough to get their papers, it is
akin to winning a lottery ticket. To refuse coming in order to wait until
the birth of a child would be like refusing a lottery ticket, and would
entail starting the whole process over again. At the Canadian Embassies
abroad people are usually told that health care in Canada is free—which
is true in every province except Ontario and British Columbia where
newcomers have to wait three months before receiving health insurance
(CCLA; Ontario Ministry of Health and Long-Term Care). These are
also the two provinces where most newcomers arrive because of large
immigrant communities for support. Toronto receives about 55,000 new
immigrants a year, ten percent from India alone, with a large proportion
being women of childbearing age (Statistics Canada). Fatima's story is
surprisingly common and yet there is no integrated health care strategy
to support women in her position. Like all other South Asian immigrants
I work with, she arrives in Canada completely naïve of the gaps in our
health care system. Being pregnant and a recent immigrant, she feels ut-
terly lost and alone—and yet thousands of women face the same plight
here, year after year (Caulford).

In order to understand how Fatima and women like her enter my care,
it is important to understand our current health care system. On arrival,
when pregnant, many women seek out medical care. Because there is such
a shortage of family physicians and because most family physicians do
not do pregnancy care, this often means they end up at a walk-in clinic
(Bringer, Maxted and Graves; Buske). While the walk-in clinic may see

someone for one visit, they do not do continuous care and would refer pregnant women to an obstetrician. Obstetricians, practicing on a fee for service basis, often require a retainer to care for uninsured women. Most obstetricians will require $2,000-$5,000 up-front before doing any clinical care—the rationale for this being that they do not want to provide services and then not be paid (Crawford). At the end of care, some of the money may be refunded depending on the services rendered.

Community Health Centers on the other hand, like midwives, are funded to provide services to all residents regardless of immigration status (Ontario Ministry of Health). However, these centers rapidly fill up and are unable to take new patients. There are also waiting lists for many midwifery clinics, but when women are transferred out of care for medical reasons, or move to another area, there may be spots that open up for women later in pregnancy. In addition, some midwifery clinics have policies where they prioritize uninsured women with the understanding that these women have limited access to the health care system. Often, even without these policies in place, clinics may take on "extra" clients on compassionate grounds because they know the women have tried to get prenatal care through other avenues and financial barriers have led them to seek midwifery care. As a result, having nowhere else to turn, women like Fatima often end up at the door of their local midwifery clinic.[4]

I go on to explain to Fatima that while the cost of our care is covered, hospital fees, any lab tests or any complications resulting in the involvement of a doctor would not be free. If she has a normal delivery in the hospital, she would have to pay in the range of $1,500. However, in the event that she ends up needing a cesarean section this can result in her needing to pay somewhere in the range of $5,000-8,000 (Crawford). Hearing this, she begins to cry again. "Why do they say Canada is the land for immigrants? How do they want us to build a life here? My husband got points on his immigration because he is a dentist but now we are here they say they won't even accept his education. He is working in a factory.... Please, please by the grace of god may this child be healthy and may this pregnancy be normal."

I explain to her that if she has a homebirth then there is no cost to her, unless there is a complication that makes us have to go to the hospital. I see that she is uncomfortable with this idea, despite my reassurance about our training, emergency skills, equipment and research on the safety of homebirths. "I don't know what to do, but sister, I trust you, whatever you say is right I will believe you."

And so my ideology of informed choice is also compromised. Ideally, a woman weighs the risks and benefits of place of birth and chooses the place she is most comfortable with and that is the safest for her. I give her recommendations, but ultimately the decision is hers. I don't know how to factor into my risk/benefit analysis, her comfort of being in a hospital with her ability to feed her children and pay her rent. Moreover, she is overwhelmed, confused, and in a new land. I am the only person she has met who can navigate the health care system for her. She is putting all of her trust in me. It is a significant burden on my new midwife shoulders.

A few weeks pass and I feel that Fatima is becoming more comfortable with me. I meet her husband and discuss the same issues with him. I see their silent interaction in contemplating place of birth—he is worried he cannot be the male provider that social norms prescribe him to be, and she is worried her body will fail her and there will be complications with the pregnancy, resulting in her being an enormous financial burden on her family.

They ask me what will happen if they are unable to pay the doctors and hospital fees. I explain that care will not be refused but that hospitals are more commonly taking people to collection agencies for non-payment.[5]

This blemish on a credit record can have dire consequences for new immigrants who are trying to open up bank accounts, get credit cards, mortgages, lease cars and generally establish life in Canada. The growing number of immigrants who, without medical insurance, are unable to pay for their medical care, is resulting in increased hostility on the part of healthcare providers. Even the most generous health care providers get frustrated by the growing number of women that they must care for and accept medico-legal liability for, without getting paid for their services. On the front lines, this can mean that women in Fatima's position are treated with open hostility. I recall a case where, unable to recover her fees, one obstetrician demanded a woman give her wedding bangles up in lieu of payment. To the doctor, it was insulting that the woman could openly display wealth by wearing "extravagant jewelry" on the one hand, while saying she could not pay the doctor's fee on the other. To a South Asian new bride, to give up her wedding jewelry is deeply humiliating and a sign that she and her family are in fact destitute in this new land.

Given the reality of these choices, Fatima and her husband eventually decide to try to have their baby at home.

The day of the birth comes and Fatima pages me saying she is in labour. When I arrive at her basement apartment, I am startled by the abject poverty. The basement is damp and moldy, smelling slightly of urine. There is rat poison in the corner and the entire family of five lives in one basement room with a single bed. There is a small kitchen upstairs in what looks like an ad-hoc addition to the house—covered by corrugated siding and with concrete floors. There is a blanket on the floor and the three children and husband are lying on it sleeping. In my privileged suburban upbringing, I did not know that such poverty actually existed in our city. At the time, I am naïve enough to think perhaps Fatima is living in "exceptional" conditions. Now ten years later, I have seen many many immigrants living in similar or worse conditions. This is the new face of Canada's poor (Hulchanski).

Fatima is quietly pacing the basement when I arrive. Except for the fact that she stops every few minutes because of a contraction and her breathing gets a bit heavier, I would not know she is in labour. I ask Fatima if I can check her to see her progress. I set up my equipment and monitor Fatima and the baby as needed, but otherwise we are all silent. Her breathing gets a bit more labored and the contractions seem closer together. "It is time," she finally says." She is still wearing her long gown, without head scarf, and I realize that she may not be comfortable lying down exposed. "Would you like to deliver on the birth stool" I ask, "some women find it easier." She agrees.

I do almost the entire delivery simply by feeling with my hands and not looking. There is just a small flashlight between her legs under the gown so I can watch for bleeding or other complications. When I see she is having a hard time near the end, I guide her hand so she can touch the baby's head—which can often ground women as they work through the pain. As soon as I do this, she lets out an astonished cry—"Mera bucha, mera bucha," she repeats—"My baby, my baby." She pushes the baby out and I deliver it into her arms. She is weeping with joy, she has had a baby girl. Later when we are debriefing the birth, Fatima tells me how happy she was to touch the baby's head and have her delivered into her arms. She has never seen any of her children so soon after delivery.

After the birth, Fatima asks me if I can clean the baby because they consider the birth fluids polluted. While the feminist in me wants to contradict this, I acquiesce and give the baby a small sponge bath in the washroom. When I return to the room, I find Fatima riffling through the garbage bag of soiled linen. She is trying to salvage some of the baby blankets that were soiled at the birth. She sees me walk into the room and I can see how humiliated she is in her desperation.

The next day before my visit, I stop at a nearby thrift store and buy a bagful of clothes for the new baby. I know it may be considered a breach of professional boundaries, but I cannot help myself. They have nothing. On the way to the house, I realize that they will not accept the clothes, especially used clothes, if they think I have bought them. In order to make her more comfortable, I tell Fatima that they are clothes that my niece has grown out of. Gently, I also tell her that there is a second hand store down the street and that they can get very good cheap clothes there.

On my next visit to Fatima's house she proudly brings the baby in and says, "I must show you what I bought at that lovely store. Such nice, cute, warm baby clothes." The baby is dressed in head to toe with a fuzzy red jumpsuit with white trim, with a pointed red hat to match. "Isn't it cute?" she asks. I don't know what to say. Her five-year-old son, who has just started school, protests, "Mama you can't dress her in that—it is for Santa Claus." Her daughter is indeed dressed in a Santa Claus costume from head to toe in the middle of September. "I don't know who this Santa, Santa is that he keeps talking about ... it is a lovely jumper." Just a few weeks into school and this five-year-old has a greater understanding of western culture than his mother. I don't say anything, I just quietly giggle to myself ... remembering my own youth as a second generation South Asian trying to explain the idiosyncrasies of the west to my Indian parents. This child is going to have a long road ahead of him.

CONCLUSION

This paper is the story of one woman—Fatima—whom I created as an archetype to illustrate the struggles of South Asian women that have been in my care. The real person on whom most of this story was based, has gone on to become an example of an immigrant "success story," with home ownership and her husband starting his own business (Mehta). I do wonder though, how Fatima's story might have been different if she had had complications with her pregnancy or birth and if she had ended up owing thousands of dollars for healthcare within the first few months of her arrival in Canada.

Fatima's character is both real and imagined, but it also touches on some of the main themes of the other South Asian mothers I have cared for, that is, the sense of isolation and fear on arriving in a new country to start a new life; the experience of having each health care door slammed in your face; the sense of disillusionment of being lured to Canada on the basis of immigration points and promises of dreams, only to realize that these points do not actually secure you a job (Javed). Also, the sense of struggle faced by each parent within the relationship as each tries to fulfill their sense of obligation towards each other and their new child.

While I chose to tell the story of Fatima in this way, I could have chosen stories of any one of dozens of other South Asian women whom I have served, who struggle with fleeing abusive situations; who are forced to have abortions by their families; or who must scrape together enough money to pay for their own health care if they are uninsured. The last several years have seen dramatic changes to Canada's once liberal immigration policies. At the same time, there have been increasing concerns raised by health care practitioners and advocacy groups about the increasing levels of poverty and systemic barriers to accessing timely and adequate health care by immigrants and refugees. In particular there has been a significant provincial campaign to eliminate the three-month waiting period for Landed Immigrants, such as Fatima, so that they can have health care coverage upon arrival in Canada (Barnes; OMA). Sadly, while the government hesitates to make access to health care easier, new immigrant women continue to have their lives put in peril.

ENDNOTES

[1]It should be noted that one of the reasons midwives fought for legislation was so that midwifery care could be accessible to more women. In the old model where midwifery was not government funded, only women who were able to pay for services could obtain a midwife—resulting in mostly privileged women being able to access midwifery care. In the 15+ years since legislation, midwifery clients have become much more diverse with respect to ethnicity, class, gender, etc. The account told here is of a client I saw in my first year of practice more than 12 years ago.

[2]There are three main tenets of midwifery philosophy is Ontario. These

are continuity of care—having a known care giver throughout pregnancy, birth and the postpartum; informed choice—recognizing the woman as the primary decision maker; and choice of birth place—the belief that all women should be able to have a safe birth, attended at the location of her choice—home or hospital.

[3]Like practitioners that work at Community Health Centers, midwives are funded to care for all "residents" of Ontario regardless of immigration status. This is because midwives do not work on a "fee for service" model, like most doctors. The "fee for service" model is attached to billing the government via the Ontario Health Insurance Plan (OHIP) (see Ontario Ministry of Health).

[4]There is a paucity of research on access to care for uninsured patients, however preliminary research suggests uninsured pregnant women are much less likely to received adequate care than those with health insurance (Wilson Mitchell and Rummens).

[5]In an urgent situation, such as labour, physicians have an ethical duty to care and cannot refuse care based on insurance status. The claim that more and more hospitals are taking uninsured patients to collections is based again on anecdotal evidence as a practitioner and being involved with patient advocacy groups.

WORKS CITED

Barnes, Steve. *Time to End the Three-Month OHIP Wait Period.* Toronto: The Wellesley Institute, 2011. Print.

Bourgeault, Ivy Lynn. *Push! The Struggle for Midwifery in Ontario.* Montreal: McGill-Queen's University Press, 2006. Print.

Bourgeault, Ivy Lynn, Cecilia Benoit and Robbie Davis-Floyd, eds. *Reconceiving Midwifery.* Montreal: McGill-Queen's University Press, 2004.

Biringer, Anne, John Maxted and Lisa Graves. *Family Medicine Maternity Care: Implications for the Future.* The College of Family Physicians of Canada, 2009. Web.

Buske, Lynda. "Family Physician Shortage Estimates." Canadian Collaborative Center for Physician Resources. September 14, 2009. Web.

Canadian Civil Liberties Association (CCLA). "CCLA Supports Call to Eliminate Three Month OHIP Waiting Period." February 4 2011. Web.

Caulford, Paul. "Providing Health Care to Medically Uninsured Immigrants and Refugees "*Canadian Medical Association Journal* 174.9

(April 2006): 1253-1254. Print.

Crawford, Trish. "Special Delivery—the $5000 Baby." *The Toronto Star* 24 Sep. 2009. Print.

Hulchanski, David. "The Three Cities within Toronto: Income Polarization among Toronto's Neighborhoods 1970-2000." 2007. Accessed 19 November 2012. Web.

Javed, Noor. "A Scarborough clinic for those with no health insurance." *The Toronto Star* Monday December 12, 2011. Print.

Mehta, Krishan. *Rethinking Immigrant Success: The Case of Four South Asian Entrepreneurs in Toronto*. Toronto: University of Toronto Press, 2005. Print.

Ministry of Health and Long-Term Care. "Community Health Centers." Accessed 19 November 2012. Web.

Nestel, Sheryl. *Obstructed Labour: Race and Gender in the Re-Emergence of Midwifery*. Vancouver: University of British Columbia Press, 2006. Print.

Ontario Medical Association (OMA). "End the Three-Month Wait for OHIP: Ontario's Doctors Urge." Press Release. Accessed 20 April 2011. Web.

Ontario Ministry of Health and Long-term Care. "OHIP Coverage Waiting Period." March 29, 2011. Accessed 19 November 2012. Web.

Statistics Canada. "Population by Immigrant Status and Period of Immigration." Accessed 19 November 2012. Web.

Wilson Mitchell, Karline and Joanna Anneke Rummens. "What Do We Know? Panel Presentation Interdisciplinary Research Evidence." Seeking Solutions: Access to Health Care for the Uninsured in Canada. Ryerson University, Toronto, Canada, February 21-22, 2012. Conference presentation.

Empowering Punjabi Mothers

A Commentary on Integrated
Holistic Counselling

BALDEV MUTTA

T HE DOOR to the agency flung open and a woman walked in with her two children. She had a bounce in her step, her hair glistened as it cascaded down her back and her heels clicked on the tile floor as she smiled at everyone and shook their hands. Her joy and confidence radiated to everyone in the room. Her children giggled as staff fussed over them, hugging them and tousling their hair. She looked over at me, and I was astounded once I recognized her. Last time I saw her we were counselling her through issues of domestic violence. Her marital relationship was debilitating and she had been in a deep depression, her children showing signs of neglect. She walked over to me, took my hands in hers and thanked me, and my staff, for giving her the support she needed to turn her life around.

At Punjabi Community Health Services (PCHS), located in Malton, Ontario, we have spent over two decades addressing issues of substance abuse, mental health and family violence in the South Asian community through our integrated holistic counselling model. In this commentary, I draw on over 30 years of experience as a social worker and activist— both in Canada and India—to show how this unique counselling model developed by PCHS has empowered Punjabi women, and in particular mothers, through building their capacity, restoring their dignity and affirming their sense of self.

Punjabi mothers usually walk through the doors of our social service agency after they have exhausted all other sources of support and the issue they are dealing with is beyond their control or comprehension. Their problems may stem from domestic violence, a child protection case, trouble their child is having with school or the law, or confusion dealing with

Canadian social norms and values. Due to the cultural stigma attached to going public with a family problem, it requires courage and a great leap of faith for Punjabi women to come to a social service agency that employs people with whom they have no familial tie or familiarity. They will have first tried to consult with their extended family, community networks and traditional healers/mystics. Only if these avenues are not helpful will they give our agency a chance. Our counselling model seeks to alleviate this initial apprehension by building the trust of a woman, embarking on a holistic assessment of the problem she is facing, and attaining her active participation and support in working towards a solution.

At PCHS we have spent over two decades developing, revising, and implementing our integrated holistic counselling model to ensure that it is effective and is meeting the needs of our clients, of whom, 75 percent are immigrants from Punjab, India, and 40 percent of those are mothers. Our clients are often from small, close-knit rural communities who may not have had much interaction with Western social norms and values prior to coming to Canada. Our model has been able to penetrate the insularity of the Punjabi community and alleviate their distrust of Western forms of intervention (such as counselling) in their personal lives, through a method that rests on three key premises: the client is in control of the treatment; the service provider must adjust their clinical and community development approach to meet the client's needs; and that illness and wellness are best understood from a client's cultural perspective. What this means for us in practice, is that we are a family centred organization that is cognizant of the cultural, familial and economic constraints on the lives of the clients, and we use non-traditional means in achieving our goals.

One example of this is shown through our approach to a situation in which a mother comes to us seeking help from abuse, stemming from her husband's alcoholism, but wants to keep her family intact. Rather than prescribe to her what she should do next, we engage her in a lengthy and intensive assessment of the situation that can take up to six months and has several phases. In the first phase, we speak to her and her close family members (children, parents, in-laws, brothers and sisters, etc.) to better understand her support network, and who really is on her side in this case of family violence. At this time, the husband may or may not be willing to be engaged in the discussion. The lack of the husband's partic-ipation in the "intervention" does not deter us from helping the mother.

In the second phase, we bring her and her family to attend the least intrusive form of intervention, which is attending parenting sessions. The last two decades of experience in the community has taught us that parents would do anything for the success of their children. As soon as the parents understand the importance of learning while attending parenting sessions, the level of receptivity of "intervention" increases. The skills learned in parenting sessions demonstrate to parents the value of listening to professionals. This in turn leads mothers and reluctant fathers to seek additional help, for issues such as addictions or mental health concerns, through other programs and services provided by PCHS. It is interesting to note that when the children behave in an acceptable manner at home, even the grandparents start attending parenting sessions and seniors' programs. These programs are held in the evenings and on weekends to accommodate work schedules.

In the third phase, once the mother has built her capacity and has more awareness of her needs we sit down and assess the situation, with her playing an integral role in the development of her treatment plan. In many cases, a woman who was initially accepting the abuse, feeling helpless and defeated, makes a decision to either leave her husband or end the abuse. Either way, PCHS is able to help the woman achieve her goal. In order for her to separate from her abusive husband, the woman needs to be prepared mentally for the constant, relentless pressure she will receive from her religious and cultural community and her family to reconcile, as well as her own internalized sense of duty and obligation to her husband and family. In addition, she must be prepared to learn about decision-making. While the insidious impact of abuse on the victim manifests as the inability to make decisions, it is also exacerbated by the cultural upbringing of Punjabi women, as they are not allowed or encouraged to make their own decisions. Finally, she must be supported unconditionally during this journey while she learns to walk through the maze of systemic hurdles and legal wrangling.

On average, we support the woman for at least five years after her separation from her husband so that she can re-establish her identity and dignity in the community. Our experience teaches us that the need to support an abused Punjabi woman increases after social services have provided her with an apartment and social assistance. Her major need is to deal with the suffocating isolation and loneliness. After leaving an abusive husband she may be ostracized from her family and religious community who did not support her decision to leave, and so distance themselves from her as a way of shaming her for her behaviour. Unfortunately, no social service agency is funded to deal with the reintegration of abused women. PCHS recognized this need and has developed programs and services, which reduce the isolation and loneliness of abused women. PCHS has bi-monthly women's support group programs, parenting programs, outings, picnics, field trips and programs for children and youth.

Another example of how our integrated holistic counselling model is used to empower Punjabi mothers is through our parenting program. While some of the women in our parenting program may be from a household in which there is domestic violence, as described above, there are many women who attend because they are experiencing extreme frustration and stress, but not violence. We devised our parenting program to take a proactive approach to issues immigrant Punjabi families are facing with their children, which stem largely from the conflict between traditional Punjabi cultural values the child is learning at home, and mainstream Western cultural values the child is getting from school, peers and society. These two sets of values can be at such odds, that a child literally "flip-flops" between both cultures, acting one way at home and another way at school. This in turn can lead to confusion and conflict between children, their parents and extended family, as well as with their teachers and peers.

The eight-session parenting course covers such topics as the husband-wife relationship, the stages of acculturation, cultural differences in worldviews and parenting, communication and problem-solving. PCHS works one on one with mothers, and as is our practice, involves the spouse and/or other family members such as grandparents to join as well. As Punjabi mothers, like many others, have not been encouraged within their cultural context to ever think about themselves and their own needs as an individual, the parenting program highlights the importance of managing boundaries between themselves as mothers and their children. This means respecting their own selfhood as well as that of their growing children, while fostering self-esteem and independence in their children.

However, as mothers try to change their parenting style, additional issues arise. The spouse may not be supportive, parents-in-law may start to discipline the child in traditional ways or undermine the mother's new disciplining practices. Mothers usually want to treat their sons and daughters on an equal footing but often the mother-in-law favours and expects preferential treatment for boys. When the mother disciplines the children, the grand-parents and other family members sabotage her authority by: interfering and arguing about her strictness with the grand-children; bribing grandchildren with money; and ridiculing the mother in front of her children. This results in children using family members against each other for their own ends. All these issues can become obstacles for the mother, and can deter her from the changes she wants to make in her life, and in her family. PCHS is able to help her move forward, by nurturing the inner strength she needs to assert herself, and resist cultural and familial pressures to be subservient.

CONCLUSION

PCHS's counselling model relies heavily on engaging the entire family in the intervention. The staff begins from a position of "where the client is at." The fact that fathers are initially not involved does not deter us from engaging the rest of the family. Our experience has shown that usually the father is engaged in the interventions once some tangible positive results are seen in the children's behaviours. The key learnings are that programs must be organized at a time convenient for the clients rather than for the staff of the agency. In addition, the client has the right to attend the programs and services as long as the client feels it is necessary for him or her to do so. The "healing" is not determined by the number of sessions but rather by the progress a client is making in the treatment process.

PCHS is currently at a stage where a new generation of facilitators are being groomed from mothers who have been attending our parenting programs for several years. These facilitators are delivering our parenting program in settings where the community gathers, such as the Gurdwara (Sikh place of worship) in order to reach a broad range of families who may still have misgivings about coming to our agency for help. The facilitators are given additional training using a learner-centred adult education model and mentored in the initial stages of this work as they build their skills as facilitators. This contributes to community development because it provides a platform for mothers who have shown leadership skills to use their knowledge and experience to further influence and empower other mothers. It is a powerful technique because the facilitators have been in the same situation as the mothers they are educating in the par-enting program, and so have first-hand knowledge of how difficult it is to challenge cultural and familial pressures and create meaningful and loving relationships with their children and with themselves.

It is our hope that through our integrated holistic counselling model, the relationships we build with Punjabi mothers and support they receive from the sincere intentions of the PCHS staff, Punjabi mothers are able to continue on their path to changing their life, their family circumstances, and empowering themselves.

I would like to thank Jasjit K. Sangha for her extensive assistance in preparing this article.

Complicating Women's Work

The "Sweat and Blood" of Womb Mothers

Commercial Surrogates Redefining Motherhood in India

AMRITA PANDE

A CCORDING TO classic kinship studies, kin relations are grounded in "natural" (biological) ties that supposedly make them immutable, special, and distinct from relationships formed in other ways (such as adoption or shared residence). David Schneider (1984) was among the first scholars to challenge traditional assumptions about biological kin relations. He demonstrated that kinship theory based on Euro-American folk assumptions about the primacy of procreative ties did not necessarily apply across cultures. While Schneider's work challenged the universality of the naturalized assumptions surrounding kinship, the advent of new reproductive technologies such as in vitro fertilization, gamete donation and surrogacy provides fresh possibilities for questioning the "natural" and biological conceptualization of both kinship and motherhood. Gestational surrogacy, for instance, creates three possible "mothers": the biological mother (the woman who contributes the ovum); the gestational mother (the surrogate) and the social or intended mother (the woman who raises the child).[1]

In this chapter, based on my extensive ethnographic research on commercial gestational surrogacy in India, I uncover the creative forms of mothering ties established by the surrogates with the fetus and the baby.[2] I demonstrate that the surrogates' alternative constructions of motherhood disrupt theories of relatedness that are based solely on biology and procreation. So, too, they disrupt the patrilineal assumptions made in studies of Indian kinship. Real ties, according to the surrogates, are based not on genes or the male seed, but in shared bodily substances (blood, breast milk), as well as the labor (sweat) of gestation and of giving birth. By emphasizing the "sweat and blood" connection between

135

the baby and its "womb" mother, surrogates in India are redefining the meaning of motherhood.

SURROGACY IN INDIA

While commercial gestational surrogacy, in general, provides rich ground for exploring new challenges to the procreative basis of kinship, surrogacy in India becomes an exceptionally rich case study because of its unusual structure. The Indian case represents an especially interesting site because it is the first developing country with a flourishing industry in national and transnational commercial surrogacy. Because of the moral and ethical ambiguity surrounding surrogacy, many countries, including China, the Czech Republic, Denmark, France, Germany, Italy, Mexico, Saudi Arabia, Spain, Sweden, Switzerland, Taiwan, Turkey and some U.S. states ban surrogacy altogether. Some countries have imposed partial bans, for instance Australia (in the state of Victoria), Brazil, Hong Kong and Hungary. In Canada, Greece, South Africa, Israel and the UK, gestational surrogacy is permitted, but is subject to regulations. Then there are other countries, with no regulations at all: Belgium, Finland and India (Teman 2010). Apart from the recent spurt of surrogacy in India, commercial surrogacy is most prevalent in the state of California and also in Israel, where it is tightly controlled by the state and restricted to Jewish citizens. The Indian structure is closer to the liberal market model of surrogacy in California, where surrogacy births are primarily managed by private, commercial agencies that screen, match and regulate agreements according to their own criteria (Pande 2009).

Although commercial surrogacy was legalized in India in 2002, there are currently no laws regulating surrogacy in clinics. Fertility clinics, such as the one clinic I studied, are free to take or reject the suggestions made by the Guidelines for Accreditation, Supervision and Regulation of Assisted Reproductive Technology (ART) issued by the Indian Council for Medical research (ICMR) in 2005. In November 2010, the ICMR submitted a final set of guidelines for the ART Act to the Law Ministry. But until a law is passed, clinics can continue to work in a legal vacuum. The absence of a surrogacy law and the informal nature of contracts imply that the experiences of surrogacy as well as its impact on various actors is very different from those in other countries where commercial surrogacy is prevalent, but subject to some form of regulation (Pande 2011). Whereas surrogacy is mediated by private, commercial agencies and lawyers in California (and other states in the U.S.) and strictly controlled by the state in Israel, there are no such intermediaries in India. The doctors are the ones making the rules, and clinics in India limit the type of surrogacy to the gestational variant.

The gestational variant requires attention because it allows commercial surrogacy to become transnational. In traditional surrogacy, the surrogate provides the genetic material as well as the womb. The intended parents, therefore, are more likely to emphasize the "right" genetic makeup (race, physical characteristics, intelligence, etc.). In gestational surrogacy, however, the surrogate's genetic makeup becomes irrelevant as she provides only her womb (Spar). India is not the only country to experience a rise in transnational surrogacy. Couples from countries such as Britain, Japan, Australia and Kuwait, where surrogacy is either illegal or restricted, have hired surrogates in the U.S to bear babies for them. However, while the total cost of such transnational packages is roughly between $100,000 to $120,000 U.S. dollars, in India the package costs a third of that amount.

FIELDWORK AND METHODOLOGY

This paper is part of my larger research project on commercial surrogacy in India, for which I conducted fieldwork between 2006 and 2011. My research has included in-depth, open-format interviews with 52 surrogates, their husbands and in-laws, 12 intending parents, three doctors, three surrogacy brokers, three hostel matrons and several nurses. In addition, I conducted participant observation for ten months at surrogacy clinics and two surrogacy hostels.[3] The interviews were in Hindi and Gujarati and were conducted either in the clinic, the surrogacy hostels where most surrogates live or at their homes. I have used pseudonyms except in cases where the surrogate asked me to use their real names.

All the surrogates in this study are married, with at least one child. The ages of the surrogates range between 20 to 45 years. Except for two surrogates, all the women are from neighbouring villages. Fourteen of the women said that they were "housewives," two said they "worked at home," and the others worked in schools, clinics, farms and stores. Their education ranged from illiterate to high school-level, with the average surrogate having approximately the beginning of a middle school level of education. The median family income is about $60 per month. If we compare that to the official poverty line of Rs. 447 ($10) per person per month for rural areas and Rs. 579 ($13) a month for urban areas, 36 of my interviewees reported a family income that put them below the poverty line (Planning Commission of India). For most of the surrogates' families, the money earned through surrogacy was equivalent to almost five years of total family income, especially since many of the surrogates had husbands who were either in informal contract work or unemployed. Transnational clients hired 35 of the surrogates in this study.

While fertility clinics from several Indian cities like New Delhi, Mumbai, Bangalore, Ahmedabad and Kolkata have reported cases of surrogacy, New Hope Maternity Clinic is one of the only clinics where the doctors, nurses and brokers play an active role in the recruitment and surveillance of surrogates. The clinic has matched over 250 surrogates with couples from India and abroad. The clinic funds several surrogacy hostels where the surrogates are literally kept under constant surveillance during their pregnancy—their food, medicines, and daily activities are monitored by the medical staff (Pande 2010a, 2010b). All the surrogates live together, in a room lined with iron beds and nothing else. Husbands and family members are allowed to visit but not stay overnight. The women have nothing to do the whole day except walk around the hostel and share their woes, experiences and gossip with the other surrogates while they wait for the next injection.

"IT MAY BE HER EGGS BUT IT'S MY SWEAT AND BLOOD": THE WOMB MOTHER VERSUS GENETIC MOTHER

While dominant discourses about kinship, parenting and relatedness emphasize the immutable blood tie between a child and the child's father, ties are more fluid in practice (Daniel; Strathern; Lambert 1996, 2000). Despite the hegemony of the tie between father and child, indigenous concepts like "shared bodily substances" validate the mother-child tie. Children share bodily substances with their mother through the ingestion of the mother's blood before birth, and breast milk after birth. The sharing of substance and sustenance is assumed to entail automatically positive and affective ties. The relative contributions of mother and father in biological reproduction are also expressed in terms of these substances or body fluids—semen, blood, and milk. For instance, in the textual and oral traditions of people in India, there is a strong emphasis on the father's contribution to procreation (Böck and Raò; Hershman). This patrilineal focus can be seen in the notions of "seed" and "earth" where seed symbolizes the father's contribution and earth or field represents the role of the mother (Dube 1986). The seed contained in semen is considered the *essence* for the creation of offspring. Women are expected to behave like earth, as mere receptacles of male seed and give back the fruit, preferably male children (Fruzzetti and Ostor; Madan; Meillassoux; Dube 2001). In popular understanding as well as in Ayurveda (the indigenous system of physiology and medicine in India) semen is understood as derived from blood, being the product of the father's seed, a child inherits the *father's blood* and is therefore placed in *his* group (Kumar 2006). The mother's blood thus becomes significant in nourishing the fetus but not in imparting identity to a child (Fruzzetti and Ostor). As Lina Fruzzetti and Akos Ostor succinctly put it, "[B]lood is male, and while it is unchangeable, it is transmitted in the male line and cut off at some point in the female line" (103).

The surrogates in this study, however, maintain a very different interpretation of the blood tie and the connection between the womb mother and the baby or fetus. They not only claim that the fetus is nourished by its gestational or womb mother's blood but also emphasize that this blood/ substance tie imparts *identity* to the child. Women within the surrogacy process, in general, and the womb mothers in particular, become more than mere receptacles of male seed. Simultaneously, womb mothers are constructed as the ones with "real mothering ties," far stronger than the tie between the baby and its genetic mother.

Parvati, hired by a couple from Mumbai, is 36 and one of the oldest surrogates at the clinic. I meet Parvati immediately after a fetal reduction surgery in which one of the fetuses had to be surgically eliminated. She tells me that she was against the fetal reduction surgery,

> *Doctor madam told us that the babies wouldn't get enough space to move around and grow, so we should get the surgery. But both Nandini didi [the genetic mother] and I wanted to keep all three. We had informally decided on that. I told Doctor Madam that I'll keep one and didi can keep two. After all it's my blood even if it's their genes. And who knows whether at my age I'll be able to have more babies.*

139

Parvati thus uses her interpretation of the blood tie, "it's my blood even if their genes," to establish mothering claims on the baby. Divya makes a similar claim. But in addition to the substantial ties of blood, Divya also emphasizes the *labor* of gestation and giving birth—her "sweat" ties with the baby—as another basis for making claims on the baby. I bump into Divya right after her second ultrasound,

> *Anne, the woman from California who is hiring me (the genetic mother), wanted a girl but I told her even before the ultrasound, coming from me it will be a boy. My first two children were also boys. This one will be too. And see I was right; it is a boy!* After all they just gave the eggs, but the blood, all the sweat, all the effort is mine. *Of course it's going after me.* [emphasis added]

This sweat (labour) and the blood (substance) tie between surrogate and fetus is often advocated by the surrogates as stronger than a connection based solely on genes. Sharda is one of the few surrogates who also breastfed the baby that she delivered. This, she feels, intensifies her mothering ties with the baby.

> *I am not sure how I feel about giving the baby away to her (the genetic mother). I know it's not her fault that she could not raise her own baby (in her womb) or breastfeed him. She has kidney problems. But she does not seem to have any emotional ties or affection for him either. Did you see when the baby started crying, she kept talking to you without paying him any attention? She keeps forgetting to change his nappies. Would you ever do that if you were a real mother? When he cries I want to start crying as well. It's hard for me not to be attached. I have felt him growing and moving inside me. I have gone through stomach aches, back aches and over five months of loss of appetite! I have taken nearly 200 injections[4] in my first month here. All this has not been easy.*

According to Sharda, her substantial ties with the baby (blood and breast milk) as well as the labour and effort she has put in to gestate the baby makes her more attached to it than the genetic mother. She criticizes the genetic mother's lack of concern for the newborn baby. Sharda believes that since the genetic mother has not put in the labor of gestation and giving birth she is incapable of feeling the emotions of a "real" mother. In Sharda's interpretation, womb mothers, rather than genetic or social mothers, are the real mothers of the baby.

This re-interpretation of motherhood cannot be dismissed as illiterate women's ignorance of modern technology. The surrogates understand and recognize that they have no genetic connection with the baby, but nonetheless emphasize the ties they have with the baby because of shared substances—blood and sometimes breast milk. These shared substances not only confer identity to the baby but also become the basis for making moral claims on the baby. Finally, for both Divya and Sharda the basis for making claims on the baby is not just shared substance but the labor, the sweat of bearing the child. In the alternative constructions of motherhood by the surrogates, shared substance and the *labor* of pregnancy not only trump the mother-child tie based solely on genes, but also the semen and blood tie between the father and the child.

THERE IS NO ROLE OF THE PENIS HERE, NOW IT'S ONLY INJECTIONS! WOMB MOTHERS VERSUS GENETIC FATHERS

Feminist writers have long recognized and criticized the gendered nature of new reproductive technologies, emphasizing the use and misuse of women's bodies to meet patriarchal ends—the male need to establish the genetic tie. Some argue that new reproductive technologies privilege men's genetic desires and objectify women's procreative capacities and that surrogacy arrangements, in particular, "devalue the mother's relationship to the child in order to exalt the father's" (Roberts 249). The surrogates in this study, however, have a different take on the significance of the genetic tie and the role of men in the surrogacy process.

The surrogacy contract prohibits surrogates from having sexual relations with their husbands. The surrogates living in surrogacy hostels are under additional surveillance and have minimal contact with their husbands. Rita has become a surrogate for the second time in two years, both times for non-resident Indian couples from the U.S. She talks about her experience with the first delivery and jokes about the "emasculation" of husbands through the surrogacy process,

During my first surrogacy pregnancy, for nine months I was not allowed to do any heavy or risky work. I was not allowed to have

any relation [sex] with my husband. [She laughs] In no other circumstance would he have agreed on that but he needed the money desperately so he had to give in! I am not surprised this thing (surrogacy) is so rare. Tell me, which man will be happy in a situation like this? [Giggling] I am big, but it's not through him. To add to that injury, when I am at the hostel, he has to look after the children and even cook sometimes.

It's hard even for Patelbhai [the genetic father]. He did not even touch me, actually he hasn't even spoken to me. At least Smitadidi [the genetic mother] has seen how I live, what I do. I tell her what the baby is doing inside. She has felt it kicking. Patelbhai is a stranger for me and I am a stranger for him. And yet I am carrying his child.

Rita seems to be arguing that the process of surrogacy requires minimum contribution by the men involved, her husband and the intended father, and is consequently, emasculating for them.

Parvati reiterates the irrelevant role of men within surrogacy and has a curious interpretation of the relationship between her husband and the fetus,

My husband stays with his parents nowadays. He visits me sometimes but we usually just talk on phone. We are not supposed to do anything [have sex] for the next few months so why bother? He doesn't need to be here. See, with your husband's child there is a constant relation, every night there is a "process" [she makes a gesture with her hands to show penetration] and this makes the seed grow inside the womb. The small seed swells up like this [she mimics a balloon being inflated by a pump] and in nine months is ready to be out. But with surrogacy there is no contact with either your husband or the other male [the biological father] so the child has to be grown by giving me injections.

Parvati argues that her husband's role or the penis's role has been taken over by medicines and technology—an injection in the case of surrogacy. While Parvati's narrative can be read as an illiterate woman's ignorance of science and biology, the implications of her narratives cannot be trivialized. By de-emphasizing her husband's role within the surrogacy process, Parvati is implicitly reiterating her contribution.

Regina uses a similar argument to justify her control over the money earned through surrogacy. Regina is a 45-year-old woman carrying the baby for a non-resident Indian from Dubai.

Oh no, I haven't talked to my husband about the money or what to do with it. Why would I? I'm the one earning it. If I tell him about it, he'll spend it. Women have to bear so much of sadness for this, why should they give the money to their husbands? And in any case what does he have to do in this? He did nothing. *At least the other man gave his sperm, not that that is a very big task either.* [emphasis added]

In *Recreating Motherhood: Ideology and Technology in a Patriarchal Society*, Barbara Katz Rothman talks about new procreative technologies strengthening the patriarchal ideology of the genetic tie—the patriarchal focus on the seed.

And so we have women, right along with men, saying that what makes a child one's own is the seed, the genetic tie, the 'blood'. And the blood they mean is not the real blood of pregnancy and birth, not the blood of the pulsating cord, the bloody show, the blood of birth, but the metaphorical blood of the genetic tie. (45)

The surrogates in this study seem to be doing exactly what women in Rothman's study are not: emphasizing the real blood of pregnancy and birth and the sweat of their labor. The male actors involved in surrogacy may have provided the seed, but their kin ties with the baby are undermined because the labor, the effort put in by them within the actual *process* of giving birth is minimal. According to the surrogates, the real ties are based on the sweat, blood and substantial connectedness between the womb mother and the baby. Such reinterpretation of relatedness and motherhood not only challenge patriliny but also allow the women to reiterate their primary role in the surrogacy process and consequently, lay claim to at least some of the money earned through surrogacy.

Such redefinitions of mothering ties that challenge patriliny, however, coexist with other narratives, which reinstate the patrilineal and patrilocal focus of kin relations in India and reify the differential roles of mothers and fathers. While the emphasis on "sweat and blood" ties between the baby and the womb mother is a powerful example of creative practices of motherhood, they do not completely subvert patriarchal assumptions about relatedness and "ownership." In India, kin ties are often based on the twin notions of patrilineality and patrilocality—descent follows the male line, girls reside with their father before marriage and husband's kin after marriage and, are considered the 'property' of their father and then their husband. The surrogates recognize and validate these assumptions.

Jyoti, hired by an Indian couple residing in the United States, reasons that the act of giving the baby away will be painful, but she is prepared for it.

> *Of course, I'll feel sad while giving her away. But then I'll also have to give up my daughter once she gets married, won't I? She is* paraya dhan *[someone else's property] and so is this one. Our girls just live with us temporarily. Their real home is with their husband and in-laws. We don't have any right over them, even though we are responsible for them. My daughter is my responsibility for 18 years, and then I have to give her up. But I still remain responsible for anything if she does something wrong. At least with this child I won't be responsible once I give her up. She will be her father's headache.*

Jyoti compares the act of giving up the surrogate baby to giving away a daughter at marriage. Indian mothers, she argues, are prepared to send daughters away to their "real" home—that of their husband and in-laws—and the surrogate baby would be nothing different. Hetal, a 35-year-old surrogate for a couple from Jaipur, echoes the same sentiment.

> *I don't think it will be hard giving her away. She is, after all, his property. He is investing so much money in her. We give away our daughters at marriage as well, don't we? Right from the day she is born we start preparing to give her away. We think she was never ours but still we do care for her when she is with us. It will be exactly the same. We know the baby is not ours; they are investing so much money, on my food, my medicines. It's their property. But I will love her like my own. That's the least I can do for them.*

Hetal labels the surrogate child the genetic father's "property," property that he has invested in and rightfully owns. Hetal vows to love the baby like her own in return for all the money invested in her medicine, food and living.

While the surrogates' experience and interpretation of ties with the baby cannot be seen as a straightforward challenge to either patriliny or patrilocality, they do seem to indicate the multivocality of kinship. On the one hand, the reinterpretation of mother-child tie by Divya, Parvati and Sharda questions the assumption that genes are the sole basis for making claims on the baby. More powerfully this re-interpretation is a subversion of hegemonic claims that the child is a product of the father's "seed" and inherits the *father's* blood. Surrogates claim the exact opposite: the child is a product of its gestational mother's blood and a fruit of all the labor and effort of gestation and this confers identity on the child. On the other hand, surrogates like Jyoti and Hetal, by invoking the genetic parents "investment," reiterate the patrilineal claim that children are their father's "property." Finally, by assimilating surrogacy into the model of giving away daughters when they get married, the surrogates are extending their claims to motherhood while at the same time acknowledging patrilocality.

INTERPRETING THE REINTERPRETATIONS: WOMB MOTHERS AS REAL MOTHERS?

Unarguably, commercial surrogacy, in which a woman agrees to waive her parental rights in exchange for payment, is a cultural anomaly (Teman 2006). It commodifies and hence threatens the traditional understanding of families as purely grounded in love, marriage, and sexual intercourse (Schneider 1968). It also shatters the assumption of a pure and complete maternal role: the genetic mother gives birth to and raises the child. The surrogates' everyday redefinition of motherhood and attempts to forge mothering ties with the baby can be seen as strategies to counter the anomalous nature of surrogacy. Despite its powerful challenges to hegemonic definitions of fatherhood and motherhood, it would be facile to end this chapter without acknowledging the irony of the redefinition of motherhood by the surrogates. The surrogates challenge the sanctity of biology and genes within a system that is an ultimate celebration of the genetic tie. The high demand for gestational surrogacy is precisely because the genetic tie remains a powerful and enduring basis of human attachment. People are ready to travel halfway across the world and hire an Indian surrogate because, unlike traditional surrogacy or transnational adoption, gestational surrogacy ensures the continuation of genetic ties. In the end, the surrogates' motherhood claims on the baby don't prevent it from being taken away from them—very often, immediately after birth.

ENDNOTES

[1]There are two types of surrogacy: the first, called traditional surrogacy, involves the surrogate being artificially inseminated with the intended father's sperm. The second, termed gestational surrogacy, is done through in vitro fertilization, in which the egg of the intended mother or of an anonymous donor is fertilized in a petri dish with the sperm of the intended father or of a donor and the embryo is transferred to the surrogate's uterus. All the cases in this study are gestational surrogacies; that is, the surrogate has no genetic connection with the baby.

[2]The origin of the term "surrogacy" and its social and political implications have been widely discussed by feminists (Stanworth; Snowdon; Rothman). Generally, a surrogate is defined as a substitute or a replacement, implying that the surrogate is a substitute mother. Critics have argued that this terminology suggests that the woman who is paid to give birth is somehow less than a mother and that this disparages her efforts and objectifies her by reducing her to her reproductive capabilities. Although the phrase "women who give birth for pay" or "womb mothers" may be preferred over the term "surrogates," in this article I use "surrogacy" and "surrogate" for purposes of brevity and clarity. The women refer to one another as "surrogate mothers," and when I explained what the term "surrogate" meant in English, most agreed that the description was fitting.

[3]There are a handful of surrogates, who live very close to the clinic, who were permitted to return home for the second trimester of pregnancy. But in almost all cases the doctor requires the surrogate to stay in surrogacy hostels where their health, diet and activities can be monitored. I should add, that surrogates sometimes prefer this arrangement since surrogacy is a very stigmatized occupation and most do not reveal to their village/ community that they are acting as surrogates. The hostels are a convenient hiding place for them for the months of pregnancy.

[4]Gestational surrogacy is a much more complex medical process than traditional surrogacy, since the surrogate is not genetically related to the

baby and her body has to be 'prepared' for artificial pregnancy. The transfer of the embryo itself is not very difficult but the process of getting the surrogate ready for that transfer and the weeks after that require heavy medical intervention. First, birth-control pills and shots of hormones are required to control and suppress the surrogate's own ovulatory cycle and then injections of oestrogen are given to build her uterine lining. After the transfer, daily injections of progesterone are administered until her body understands that it is pregnant and can sustain the pregnancy on its own. The side effects of these medications can include hot flashes, mood swings, headaches, bloating, vaginal spotting, uterine cramping, breast fullness, light-headedness and vaginal irritation.

WORKS CITED

Böck, Monica and Aparna Rao. "Indigenous Models and Kinship Theories: An Introduction to a South Asian Perspective." *Culture, Creation and Procreation: Concepts of Kinship in South Asian Practice*. Eds. Monica Böck and Aparna Rao. New York: Berghahn Books, 2000. 1-52. Print.

Daniel, E. Valentine. *Fluid Signs: Being a Person the Tamil Way*. Berkeley: University of California Press, 1984. Print.

Dube, Leela. "Seed and Earth: The Symbolism of Biological Reproduction and Sexual Relations of Production." *Visibility and Power*. Eds. Leela Dube, Eleanor Leacock and Shirley Ardener. Delhi: Oxford University Press, 1986. 22-53. Print.

Dube, Leela. *Anthropological Explorations in Gender: Intersecting Fields*. New Delhi: Sage Publications, 2001. Print.

Fruzzetti, Lina and Akos Ostor. *Kinship and Ritual in Bengal: Anthropological Essays*. New Delhi: South Asian Publisher Pvt. Ltd. 1984. Print.

Hershman, Paul. *Punjabi Kinship and Marriage*. Delhi: Hindustan Publishing Corporation, 1981. Print.

Kumar, Pushpesh. "Gender and Procreative Ideologies Among the Kolams of Maharashtra." *Contributions to Indian Sociology* 40.3 (2006): 280-309. Print.

Lambert, Helen. "Caste, Gender and Locality in Rural Rajasthan." *Caste Today*. Ed. C. J. Fuller Delhi: Oxford University Press, 1996. 93-123. Print.

Lambert, Helen. "Village Bodies? Reflection on Locality, Constitution, and Affect in Rajasthani Kinship." *Culture, Creation and Procreation:*

Concepts of Kinship in South Asian Practice. Eds. Monica Böck and Aparna Rao. New York: Berghahn Books, 2000. 81-100. Print.

Madan, T. N. "The Ideology of the Householder Among the Kashmiri Pandits." *Contributions to Indian Sociology* 15.1,2 (1981): 223–50. Print.

Meillassoux, Claude. *Maidens, Meals and Money.* Cambridge: Cambridge University Press, 1981. Print.

Pande, Amrita. *Commercial Surrogate Mothering in India: Nine Months of Labor?* Ph.D. Dissertation, University of Massachusetts, Amherst, 2009. Print.

Pande, Amrita. "Commercial Surrogacy in India: Manufacturing a Perfect 'Mother-Worker'." *Signs* 35.4 (2010a): 969-994. Print.

Pande, Amrita. "'At Least I Am Not Sleeping with Anyone': Resisting the Stigma of Commercial Surrogacy in India." *Feminist Studies* 36.2 (2010b): 292-314. Print.

Pande, Amrita. "Transnational Commercial Surrogacy in India: Gifts for global sisters?" *Reproductive Biomedicine* 23.5 (November 2011): 618-625. Web.

Planning Commission of India. "Report of the Expert Group to Review the Methodology for Estimation of Poverty." 2009. Accessed 30 May 2011. Web.

Roberts, Dorothy E. *Killing the Black Body: Race, Reproduction, and the Meaning of Liberty.* Pantheon Books: New York, 1997. Print.

Rothman, Barbara Katz. *Recreating Motherhood: Ideology and Technology in a Patriarchal Society.* New York: W. W. Norton, 1989. Print.

Schneider, David Murray. *American Kinship: A Cultural Account.* Chicago: University of Chicago Press, 1968. Print.

Schneider, David Murray. *A Critique of the Study of Kinship.* Ann Arbor: University of Michigan Press, 1984. Print.

Snowdon, C. "What Makes a Mother? Interviews With Women Involved in Egg Donation and Surrogacy." Birth 21.2 (1994): 71-84. Print.

Spar, D. L. *The Baby Business: How Money, Science, and Politics Drive the Commerce of Conception.* Cambridge, MA: Harvard Business School Publishing Corporations, 2006. Print.

Stanworth, Michelle. "Reproductive Technologies and the Deconstruction of Motherhood." *Reproductive Technologies: Gender, Motherhood, and Medicine.* Cambridge: Polity, 1987. 10-35. Print.

Strathern, Marilyn. *The Gender of the Gift: Problems with Women and*

Problems with Society in Melanesia. Berkeley: University of California Press, 1988. Print.

Teman, Elly. *The Birth of a Mother: Mythologies of Surrogate Motherhood in Israel.* Ph.D. Dissertation, Dept. of Sociology and Social Anthropology, The Hebrew University of Jerusalem, 2006.

Teman, Elly. *Birthing a Mother: The Surrogate Body and the Pregnant Self.* Berkeley: University of California Press, 2010. Print.

Perspectives on Work and Family Lives

Exploring the Lived Experiences of South Asian Immigrant Mothers Working from Home in Toronto

SRABANI MAITRA

"You want to know how my whole day looks like? Really? [Jennifer laughs out loud], hmmm ... let me think.... I get up at 5:00 in the morning and go straight to the kitchen to put the kettle on the stove. Between 5:00 and 5:30, I enjoy the serenity while my husband and children sleep in the bedroom. I also plan what to cook for the day.... From 5:30 to 6:00 or 6:15 I prepare breakfast and then wake up my kids who have to get ready to go to school. Then I prepare the lunch, take a shower, and get ready for my kids to come back home around noon. If there's any other chores like cleaning I will finish them then. My husband then gets ready to leave, as he has a part-time job before going to his regular evening shift. I try to finish all my stitching in the evening.... My husband comes back at 11:00, we eat, watch TV together or chat, and then by 12:00 we go to bed. On weekends when he is home I don't do much housework. I just concentrate on my business work. Between us, we have lot of understanding and love and I think in this country, as immigrants ... where every minute you have to worry about money and survival, as a family we are happy and content."

THIS IS JENNIFER, a mother of two. She has a graduate degree in Child Psychology from Sri Lanka where she was a Montessori teacher for five years. Unable to find any teaching positions after migration, she currently stitches and sells baby clothes and runs a small home-based daycare.

As the above passage elucidates "motherwork" (Collins 2000) can be exhausting. Jennifer's story raises several issues of interest concerning not only the amount of everyday activities a mother does in relation to household tasks and care giving but also the dynamics of intra-family relationships vis-à-vis social expectations placed on women's roles as mothers in the context of immigration. This paper examines how South Asian immigrant mothers negotiate their mothering, migrant status and home-based work, while being situated at the intersections of gender, race and class barriers. The paper argues that the "negotiation" is evident in how these women re-define their roles as working mothers by valuing their love, nurturance and support for the family vis-à-vis their home-based work.

Feminist scholars, particularly feminists of colour have played a vital role in illuminating how motherwork, its meanings and demands, are shaped by the politics of gender, race, class and migration (Collins 1994: 209; Glenn 1994: 7). While acknowledging the fact that women of colour are often subjected to gender domination, they call for a deconstruction of the archetypal portrayals of men as typically "patriarchal" and women as the "oppressed," "dependent" and "passive" home maker (Glenn 1994: 3, 9). They argue that such atypical, essentialist portrayals tend to repudiate the presence of alternative and/or egalitarian family structures within many racialized communities. Such alternative family structures are important in highlighting how many women of colour, through their mother/work challenge the "social constructions of work and family as separate spheres, [and] of male and female gender roles as similarly dichotomized" (Collins 1994: 47). Evelyn Nakano Glenn (1986: 187) crucially points out that these women, while performing their mothering roles, remain a source of support and nurturance for their partners as well as their families, particularly in the context of racial exploitation faced by significant populations of women and men of colour.

Along with gender and race, migration is said to further complicate the terrains of mothering, gender roles and related gendered divisions of labour. In their struggle to balance both family and work lives (sometimes for the very first time) after migration, many women of colour find themselves moving "back and forth constantly between 'public' and 'private'labour since economic provision for the family... [becomes] an expected part of mothering" (Glenn 1994: 6). Thus, as Collins argues, rather than examining mothering solely in relation to patriarchy or male domination within families and societies, what needs to be foregrounded are both "power and powerlessness" of women of colour "within an array of social institutions that frame their lives" (1994: 53; see also Park 27).

This paper adds to the literature by focusing on an important area of work that has increasingly become a reality for many immigrant women of colour in Canada—home-based work. The focus on home-based work is vital for two reasons. First, since the 1990s, women's work worldwide (including North America) has undergone an increased "informalization" as well as "domestication" due to the trade liberalization and economic recessions characterizing the global world (Giles and Preston 147; Ng 110). While "informalization" refers to non-regulated work both paid and unpaid (Giles and Preston 147), "domestication" has ushered in a "shift in the locations and sites of paid work from formal workplaces to domestic premises" (Giles and Preston 147; see also, Ng 110). While there can be a variety of home-based work ranging from paid work to businesses, the creation of such work arrangements has disproportion-ately affected immigrant women of colour who are overrepresented in the informal, low paid, precarious types of homework (Giles and Preston 150-151). Second, homework challenges any boundaries existing between the private and the public by making it malleable. By dint of being located at home, the space ideologically constructed as "women's place" (Prügl and Boris 7), homework "brings the wage into the place where 'love', 'duty', and 'need' ... compel labour" (Prügl and Boris 7).

Within the limited literature that exists on immigrant women's home-based work, most studies concentrate on gendered divisions of labour and the invisibility that home-based work shares with domestic work (Abreu and Sorj 101-107). In this context, scholars mainly argue that home-based work exacerbates women's dual responsibilities of household work and childcare (Gurstein 5). Moreover, as the separation between home and work becomes quite blurry, home-based work often loses its "professional legitimacy not only at the macro level in the hierarchy of professions but also in the perceptions of other family members" (Abreu and Sorj 101). Such underestimation is aggravated when homework is undertaken by immigrant women of colour (Ng 110), who are often assumed to be docile, and domesticated. Consequently, despite earning at home, the social organization of the women's lives remains rooted in gender/race hierarchies and an ideology of motherhood (Abreu and Sorj 101-102).

Given the limited number of studies that exist on immigrant women of colour in conjunction with work-motherhood dynamics, my study of South Asian immigrant mothers in Toronto working from home contributes to the literature on how immigrant mothers of colour balance family and work responsibilities in the host country. Concomitant with the pressures of their mothering roles they also have to adapt to shifting racial and class dynamics, issues that are often new to them and only emerge with migration. I argue that South Asian immigrant women's mothering signifies a constant "negotiation" between work and family responsibilities. This "negotiation" is evident in how these immigrant mothers endeavour to re-define their roles as working mothers in a new country circumscribed by conflicting economic forces and life trajectories.

RESEARCH METHOD

The discussions in this paper are based on my doctoral research where I conducted semi-structured, in-depth interviews with 25 immigrant women from India, Bangladesh, Pakistan and Sri Lanka living in Toronto and the Greater Toronto Area. All of them when interviewed were running small, informal businesses such as sewing or selling of garments/ ethnic clothes, catering and babysitting from home. These businesses were small, low-income, with no benefits, and in most cases unaccounted for. All the women, except one, were fluent in English, held university degrees from their home countries and had previous work experience in such areas as IT, sales or administration. They were all married, aged above 30 and, 11 out of 25 were mothers. While the small sample size of my research (11 mothers) cannot be representative of the experiences of the South Asian community residing in Toronto, it illustrates the complexities involved in how many women of colour try to manage both their work and mothering responsibilities, while coping with their lives in a new country marked by evolving relationships of race, gender and class.

EMPLOYMENT TRAJECTORY IN THE HOST COUNTRY

During my interviews with the South Asian immigrant women, one of the most important factors that came up as women discussed their post-migration experience was their inability to get employed in their own area of education and previous work experience. In this connection women reiterated two factors impeding their entry into the mainstream labour market: racial and systemic barriers in the Canadian labour market and gendered control within families.

Researchers (Galabuzi; Vosko) who have studied the linkages between immigration status, unemployment, poverty and racial origin, have demonstrated the existence of a racialized and gendered labour market in Canada where people of colour, particularly highly educated women, are overrepresented in low income sectors, characterized as a "cheap," "docile" and "flexible" labour force. These findings have been corroborated by scholars who have reported that, compared to European-born immigrant women, those from Asia, Africa and other "third world" countries experience further devaluation of their qualifications and increased barriers to high income occupations (Das Gupta 6-8; Mojab 127).

The interviewees in my project also experienced labour market barriers that vastly devalued their prior education and qualifications. Most of them complained about how often there would be no response from the employers to their job applications or they would be merely advised to acquire "Canadian work experience" and/or "Canadian education" by the immigrant serving organizations. Women often felt that their South Asian accent or skin colour may have had something to do with such underestimation, so that despite having university education from their home countries and in some cases professional degrees, they did not find any job openings appropriate to their education and work experience.

Parallel to the racialization and segmentation, women also noted another level of domination that continues to enmesh the lives of many South Asian immigrant women in Canada. This arises from the various restrictive patriarchal values, which infringe upon women's decisions to work, study, or stay at home. While patriarchal domination does not constitute the reality of every South Asian woman's life, scholars point out that many women do experience rigid patriarchal control (Martins and Reid 204) whereby they are expected to "bear most of the responsibility for providing support and sustenance to the family... and to define themselves in terms of their roles as wives and mothers" (George and Ramkissoon 114). Interestingly, although the women in my research were part of the paid workforce in their home countries, upon migration some of them found their lives complicated by increased gendered control and domination. For instance, a few interviewees reported that after migration it was the husbands who were reluctant to let their wives work while they themselves worked long hours to make ends meet. Some men would prevent their wives from looking for jobs by reminding them of their childcare and mothering responsibilities.

In analyzing the manifestation of comparatively rigid forms of gender control in the host country, scholars cite such reasons as men's lack of opportunity in the new country or the reversal of their breadwinner roles and subsequent loss of self-esteem and control over family affairs (Walton-Roberts and Pratt 188). Indeed, several respondents pointed out how many of their well-qualified spouses were either unemployed or working in factories. Some even referenced the sudden bout of anger and depression felt by their men while trying to cope with un/under employment. The women's narratives thus reveal how patriarchy can "reinvigorate itself" as it wrestles with the larger, mainstream racist and classist Canadian society (Shi 47). It is important to note here that despite referring to gender barriers, most women were of the opinion that more so than gender ideologies, it was the racial and systemic barriers prevalent in the Canadian labour market that played a much greater role in relegating them to the informal job sector. As Saadiya, a former editor from Pakistan had pointed out to me:

> *I think it is a misconception that our husbands do not want us to work. Not all husbands dislike their wives going out and working, it is also the question of opportunity. There is no opportunity for us in Canada.*

The above statement, I believe, challenges the common assumption that women of colour are unable to look for jobs in the mainstream labour market and remain tied to the informal, precarious economy, solely because of the patriarchal values that bind them to family responsibilities and motherhood. On the contrary, my research demonstrates that patriarchal control is complicated and enforced through the discounting of the women's pre-migration work experience and credentials by the Canadian labour market that affect non-white immigrant women's economic integration. This consequently results in social precariousness, downward class mobility and, in many cases, spiraling poverty. Home-based small businesses often remain their last resort to economically survive in Canada after multiple failures to enter the mainstream labour market.

Another common sentiment that was shared by many mothers was their loss of support and help that greatly increased their household and childcare responsibilities after migration. Before immigration most of these women belonged to middle class families and could have afforded domestic help in their own countries. Upon migration however, financial instability forced them to avoid day care and almost single-handedly carry out all the responsibilities. The contradictory class position that these women experienced after coming to Canada, has been analyzed by scholars like Kiran Mirchandani, who have reasoned that immigrant women's class position does not remain static and that "many are often middle-class on some dimensions and simultaneously working-class on others" (29).

Women's decision to start small businesses at home was thus contingent on their inability to get jobs in their own fields as well as gendered expectations of spouses and families. Often forced to stay at home, something most women never anticipated doing before, their work from home was thus a way to negotiate the constraints they were facing in the labour market and sometimes at home.

VALUES OF MOTHERING

Torn between the role of a primary caregiver with major household responsibilities and a willingness to participate in the labour force, how do South Asian women then view their role as mothers? According to Sayantani DasGupta and Shamita Das DasGupta (113), mothers hold a special position in South Asian cultures and are vested with huge responsibilities in terms of socialization of their children. The iconized mother figure is often glorified as one who is self-sacrificing, selfless and dedicated to the duties of childrearing and the household (Jeffery 225). However, in such cases where women have to constantly "shift gears" to manage their work and home spaces, scholars call attention to how many mothers remain fraught with the constant tensions about their abilities to carry on the role of a "good" mother: "being ever present to shower love, provide care, stimulate and educate the child, and more—while attempting to be good workers as well" (Devasahayam and Yeoh 13).

In my research, the predominant sentiment was the value and pride women took in their mothering work. For those mothers who were mainly working from home, spending time with their children was one of the most important elements of their mother work. Jennifer was happy working from home as she could take care of her children and did not have to leave them at a day care all the time. She felt that she should devote most of her time to her husband and especially children when they are growing up:

> This is the time when they need me... they are young and when I go out even for 20 minutes they start missing me because I am always there. I think it's a precious time, seeing them growing up and enjoying time with them. I tell my husband all the time what he is missing.

Devoting time for family and children was also borne out of the fact that many women did not have the jobs they desired and were unwilling to be in part-time casual work. When forced to work from home, many mothers thus preferred to be the primary caregiver rather than working in low paid, part-time jobs that they felt would do nothing to enhance their career. Thaya shared a similar experience. She said:

> My baby is getting good life because I am staying at home. I am taking care of the baby. I stay home. What's the use of working so hard in a soap factory? At least I am working for my own family here.

Furthermore, many women spoke about how the expenses and lack of proper childcare programs put pressure on women to take care of their home and children. Zarine, a former bank secretary from Pakistan, commented about this:

> You know the thing is people tell me that if I join a factory I will be earning 800/900 but that will be what I will spend for babysitting for my four kids so what's the use of working then? It's better then that I look after my kids. I need to spend time with my kids.

Thus, generally, women felt that in the absence of any job suitable to their qualifications, they would at least fulfil the duties of a "good mother." This consisted of a clear understanding of what their children needed, what they were doing after school, keeping track of their educational progress and creating a harmonious life for them in the host country.

What can be gleaned from the above discussions is that most South Asian women felt that as mothers it was their primary responsibility to care for their children. This belief in their role as mothers can perhaps be explained by the continuation of traditional patriarchal beliefs that hold women responsible for caregiving and nurturance. At the same time, this gendered ideology is ratified by the lack of job opportunities so that women become primarily responsible for housework and childcare along with being implicated in the perpetuation of cultural beliefs centered on mothering as part of their "normal" duty. However, women's decision to work from home and care for their families rather than getting subsumed by the precarious labour market that thrives on their cheap labour, is also an indication of how women immigrants try to challenge the appropriation of their surplus labour by choosing to base their lives on love, care, nurturance (Bayat 548-549) and support for the family members.

NEGOTIATING MOTHERING AND HOME-BASED WORK

Although the South Asian immigrant women were working in non-standard, precarious sectors far below their qualifications with their lives enmeshed by racial segregation, strict gender ideologies, and mothering responsibilities, they were actively involved in a struggle and negotiation to create their own identity as mothers and workers. Two important areas can be identified in this context. First, women were active in negotiating patriarchal control and gendered divisions of labour. For instance, in those cases where women were not allowed by their husbands to look for jobs because of their children and domestic responsibilities, many women reasoned with their spouses to convince them of the necessity for them to work. As Rumona, who runs a day care reflected:

> My husband didn't approve of me also working. But I knew that my husband alone cannot buy a house here or a car. We cannot provide good education to our children either. So I waited and reasoned with him that if I work everything will be much better. It took time but he agreed. So then we both talked and then he told that yes it is important that you work and we can make more money and have a better life.

Others successfully reorganized housework and child care at home. Saadiya mentioned how she explained to her husband the amount of work she has to put in everyday as a mother. She made him realize that despite being at home she is working more than him and it is important that he shares some of her responsibilities. Moreover, when women wanted to take a course or attend a job search workshop, they would ask their husbands to cook or take care of the children.

Women's "bargaining" with gendered expectations exemplifies how patriarchal values are not merely reconfigured, but also "transformed and renegotiated" (Walton-Roberts and Pratt 175) as people migrate from one place to the other. The imperative to find work provides them with a possibility for re-configuration of the family dynamics, even if patriarchy, as such, is not entirely displaced. The social realities of immigration and the material necessities of finding economic sustenance share a complex relationship with gender and patriarchy here, where the settled parameters of family roles during pre-immigration periods shift ineluctably after immigration. While by itself, the domain of the family does not provide succor against the "hard" disjunctures of a racialized Canadian labour market and society, the place of the family nonetheless remains a vital point of remaking immigrant person-hood, often with potentially beneficial results.

Secondly, while most women took pride in their mothering roles, at the same time, they remained engaged in their home-based businesses and took several initiatives to underscore the importance of their work both economically as well as socially. For example, most of the home-workers complained about how their work was often underestimated so that they had to take steps to change the attitude of their families towards their work. That is to say, paid work becomes a crucial point of bargaining the very basis of family ties in addition to re-defining the mother's role in such a family milieu. Shashi, a former financial analyst running a catering service described her situation to me:

> My family never took my work seriously. They would always make plans I used to give in to without considering my work. But then when my business became bigger I had to step up. I would purposely not cook or clean and let my husband do that. Once when the kids were planning to go for a vacation I refused to accompany them because of my work load. This gradually

*made them realize that they cannot take my work for granted.
My income is crucial to the family.*

While working from home, women were also aware of the lack of social participation they were experiencing in their new country. Therefore, many of them started home-based businesses not merely out of necessity but also to connect with other women and to be able to continue with their social lives in whatever way possible. Sabitha shared her feelings with me:

*Between my friends we organize potluck every month, go watch
a movie together or go for shopping. My husband knows that I
will not do any work that day and he will have to manage the
kids and also the house. That is my day when I enjoy with my
friends. We also help each other in many different ways when
it comes to running our businesses.*

Apart from fostering a semblance of community life, these informal networks of communication that women establish with each other, therefore, also become vital nodal points for exchanging possibilities of finding work and economically productive activities.

Thus, what becomes evident from the narratives above is how South Asian mothers challenge and struggle in contexts where various social processes and forms of stratifications impede their acceptability and development in mainstream Canadian society. Situated at the intersections of racialized barriers and patriarchal control, the women experience complex challenges. On the one hand, they are driven by their aspirations to work and build their careers, often thwarted by racial and systemic discrimination existing in the Canadian labour market. On the other hand, they wish to sustain and nurture their families as mothers and wives; yet have to ensure a minimum level of economic survival to be able to do so. In this paper I argued, that under the effects of these two divergent challenges, women remake their personhood as well as intra-family gender dynamics through strategic bargaining of their economic activities centered around home-based work.

WORKS CITED

Abreu, Alice Rangel de Paiva and Bila Sorj. "Good Housewives: Seamstresses in the Brazilian Garment Industry." *Homeworkers in Global Perspective: Invisible No More*. Eds. Eileen Boris and Elisabeth Prügl. New York: Routledge, 1996. 93-110. Print.

Bayat, Asef. "From 'Dangerous Classes' to 'Quiet Rebels': Politics of the Urban Subaltern in the Global South." *International Sociology* 15.3 (2000): 533-557. Print.

Collins, Patricia Hill. "Shifting the Center: Race, Class, and Feminist Theorizing About Motherhood." *Mothering: Ideology, Experience, and Agency*. Eds. Evelyn Nakano Glenn, Grace Chang and Linda Rennie Forcey. New York, London: Routledge, 1994. 45-66. Print.

Collins, Patricia Hill. *Black Feminist Thought: Knowledge, Consciousness, and the Politics of Empowerment*. 2nd ed. New York: Routledge, 2000. Print.

DasGupta, Sayantani and Shamita Das DasGupta. "Sex, Lies, and Women's Lives: An Intergenerational Dialogue." *A Patchwork Shawl: Chronicles of South Asian Women in America*. Ed. Shamita Das DasGupta. New Brunswick, NJ: Rutgers University Press, 1998. 111-128. Print.

Das Gupta, Tania. *Racism and Paid Work*. Toronto: Garamond Press, 1996. Print.

Devasahayam, Theresa and Brenda S. A. Yeoh. "Asian Women Negotiating Work Challenges and Family Commitments." *Working and Mothering in Asia: Images, Ideologies and Identities*. Eds. Theresa Devasahayam and Brenda S. A. Yeoh. Singapore: NIAS Press, 2007. 3-28. Print.

Galabuzi, Grace-Edward. "Social Exclusion: Socio-Economic and Political Implications of the Racialized Gap." *Daily Struggles: The Deepening Racialization and Feminization of Poverty in Canada*. Eds. Maria A. Wallis and Siu-Ming Kwok. Toronto: Canadian Scholars' Press Inc, 2008. 81-94. Print.

George, Usha, and Sarah Ramkissoon. "Race, Gender, and Class: Interlocking Oppressions in the Lives of South Asian Women in Canada." *AFFILIA* 13.1 (Spring1998): 102-119. Print.

Giles, Wenona and Valerie Preston. "The Domestication of Women's Work: A Comparison of Chinese and Portuguese Immigrant Women Homeworkers." *Studies in Political Economy* 51 (1996): 147-181. Print.

Glenn, Evelyn Nakano. *Issei, Nisei, War Bride: Three Generations of Japanese American Women in Domestic Service*. Philadelphia: Temple University Press, 1986. Print.

Glenn, Evelyn Nakano. "Social Constructions of Mothering: A Thematic

Overview." *Mothering: Ideology, Experience, and Agency*. Eds. Evelyn Nakano Glenn, Grace Chang and Linda Rennie Forcey. New York, London: Routledge, 1994. 1-32. Print.

Gurstein, Penny. *Wired to the World, Chained to the Home: Telework in Daily Life*. Vancouver: University of British Columbia Press, 2001. Print.

Jeffery, Patricia. "Agency, Activism and Agendas." *Appropriating Gender: Women's Activism and Politicized Religion in South Asia*. Eds. Patricia Jeffery and Amrita Basu. New York, London: Routledge, 1998. 221-244. Print.

Martins, Vanessa and Denise Reid. "New-Immigrant Women in Urban Canada: Insights into Occupation and Sociocultural Context." *Occupational Therapy International* 14.4 (2007): 203-220. Print.

Mirchandani, Kiran. "A Special Kind of Exclusion: Race, Gender and Self-Employment." *Atlantis* 27.1 (Fall/Winter 2002): 25-37. Print.

Mojab, Shahrzad. "De-Skilling Immigrant Women." *Canadian Woman Studies/les cahiers de la femme* 19.3 (1999): 123-128. Print.

Ng, Roxana. "Homeworking: Dream Realized or Freedom Constrained? The Globalized Reality of Immigrant Garment Workers." *Daily Struggles: The Deepening Racialization and Feminization of Poverty in Canada*. Eds. Maria A. Wallis and Siu-ming Kwok. Toronto: Canadian Scholars' Press, 2008. 95-102. Print.

Park, Keumjae. "'I Can Provide for My Children': Korean Immigrant Women's Changing Perspectives on Work Outside the Home." *Gender Issues* 25.1 (2008): 26-42. Print.

Prügl, Elisabeth, and Eileen Boris. "Introduction." *Homeworkers in Global Perspective: Invisible No More*. Eds. Eileen Boris and Elisabeth Prügl. New York, London: Routledge, 1996. 3-18. Print.

Shi, Yu. "The Formation of a Chinese Immigrant Working-class Patriarchy: Reinventing Gendered Expectations within the Structural Confines of U.S. Society." *Meridians: Feminism, Race, Transnationalism* 9.1 (2008): 31-60. Print.

Vosko, Leah F. "Precarious Employment: Towards an Improved Understanding of Labour Market Insecurity." *Precarious Employment: Understanding Labour Market Insecurity in Canada*. Ed. Leah F. Vosko. Quebec: McGill-Queen's University Press, 2006. 3-40. Print.

Walton-Roberts, Margaret, and Geraldine Pratt. "Mobile Modernities: A South Asian family negotiates immigration, gender and class in Canada." *Gender Place and Culture* 12.2 (2005): 173-195. Print.

Iconic Mothering, Outlaw Mothering

Selfless to Selfish

Trajectory of "Mother" from Bollywood's *Mother India* to *Pyar Mein Twist*

AMBER FATIMA RIAZ

T HIS PAPER will trace the changing representations of the mother figure in Indian film, beginning with the 1957 film *Mother India*, which attained canonical status for its representation of womanhood and motherhood and ending with a comparison to the 2005 movie *Pyar Mein Twist* (A Twist in a Love Story). As I trace the trajectory of filmic representations of the "mother figure" in Hindi cinema, [1] I will show that although Bollywood moves from representations of the "mother" as the ultimate, selfless nurturing figure to focus on the needs and desires of the mother herself, the image of the mother as a self-sacrificing, perfect home-builder is not rejected completely. I argue that the changing representations of motherhood in films like *Pyar Mein Twist* in which a mother of grown children finds a new love interest/husband for herself (a radical storyline for Bollywood) are attempts to strike a balance between the "classic" Indian virtues represented in *Mother India* and the demands of Bollywood's new audience—the "modern" transnational/ global Indian diaspora.

The film, *Mother India*, was released in 1957, and was "self-consciously epic and nationalist" (Roy 112). It was three years in the making, and once released, ran for 50 weeks in Bombay alone. It was the first Indian movie to be nominated for an Oscar for best foreign language film, and the lead actress, Nargis, won an award for best actress in the Filmfare awards (India's equivalent to the Oscars) (Roy 112). The film is said to have played continuously in some part or other of India since its release, and is considered to be one of the classics of Indian cinema. Its success turned the lead actress into an iconic embodiment of ideal femininity and sacrificial motherhood.

The film revolves around the story of Radha (played by Nargis), and begins with her marriage to Shamu (played by Raj Kumar). The wedding is paid for by a loan, the conditions of which are such that both Radha and Shamu have to pay three quarters of their annual crop to the money-lender, Sukhilal, in interest. In trying to use more of the arid parts of their land, Shamu's arms are crushed, and he becomes completely dependent on his wife. He sees the loss of his arms as a loss of his own "manhood" and literally walks away from his family, leaving Radha pregnant with three young boys to tend to. Radha continues to work the land. After persuading the villagers to re-build their village following devastating floods she becomes the "mother" of the village. Even though the villagers re-build, Sukhilal's exorbitant interest rates make it impossible for them to alleviate their poverty. The moneylender offers to write off Radha's loans if she agrees to become his mistress, but she refuses, deeming her chastity to be more important. The film then skips forward a number of years, and Radha is shown with grown sons. Consumed by the need for revenge against Sukhilal, whom he holds responsible for his family's abject poverty, the youngest son becomes a bandit, and attempts to ab-duct and rape the moneylender's daughter in order to get back at him for all the years of hardship. Radha kills him, for the rape of Sukhilal's daughter would have been the rape of the village's daughter, and honour and chastity must be upheld at any cost.

The figure of woman/mother presented within the film is that of the chaste, honourable, eternally patient mother, one who will willingly sac-rifice her own son in the name of honour, and one who does not need a man for protection. If anything, the husband is an unnecessary addition, someone who can be forgotten once he has fulfilled his role of providing Radha with sons. She has come to represent the values of Indian nation-alism and of motherhood, embodying the highly valued concepts of *laaj/ izzat*[2] [chastity/honour]. The mother figure here weathers many storms, endures poverty, even abandonment, in order to keep her family—and by extension an entire village—together. In return, she expects them to remain forever loyal and faithful. Interestingly, in *Mother India*, the sacrifice is made for male children. She is not "burdened" by the birth of girls, and is instead "blessed" by not one, but four sons. I am gesturing here to the politics of gender intrinsic to Indian social arrangements, one commonly held belief of which is the idea that a girl will marry and leave the family while a son will take care of the aging mother. The opening scene of the film shows Radha flanked by her last remaining son and his wife and children, loved, respected and honoured by both the villagers and the "good" son. Even though two of her sons die in the floods that destroy the village in the first half of the film, and she herself kills her youngest son, she is able to enjoy her old age in peace because her "good" and obedient son still survives to take care of her.

Radha is a complex characterization of "goddess mother" invoking a number of goddesses from the Hindu Pantheon[3] that, in turn, underscores the dramatic impact and experience of the film itself. As Rosie Thomas has shown in her article "Sanctity and Scandal: The Mythologization of Mother India," Radha represents:

> Sita (archetypal dutiful, loyal wife and embodiment of purity, whose trial by fire and abandonment with two young sons are implicitly invoked; Savitri (exemplarily devoted wife); Radha herself (the cowherd who was Krishna's lover); Lakshmi (goddess of wealth and good fortune, to whom brides are customarily likened and to whom Sukhilal [the moneylender in Mother India] explicitly, and somewhat ironically, given the context of his attempted seduction, likens Radha); and the more fearsome mother goddesses, Durga and Kali, powerful symbols of female sacred authority and embodiments of shakti (female power), who punish and destroy if they are displeased. There are also more covert references, for example, to Surabai, the holy cow, and to Mother Earth, the fertility principle. (17)

Given the complexity of the images and emotions invoked, it is no wonder, then, that the film's construction of femininity, sexual power, chastity and devoted motherhood dominated Hindi cinema for decades, with mothers continuously represented as self-sacrificing and powerful personalities whose power of undying love and devotion gave immense strength to the male protagonists. Even in the action films of the 1980's, dominated by the "angry young man" protagonist, men continuously invoked the power of the mother's breast-milk—calling out to villains: *"agar maa ka doodh piya hai to aa kar mera saamna karo"* [if you have drunk mother's milk then come out and face me like a man].

The film brings to the forefront issues of womanhood, and of motherhood, as well as the iconicity of "mother" as "nation." Vijay Mishra, in his book chapter "The Texts of 'Mother India'," has shown that the iconicity of Nargis's portrayal stems from the quintessential trope of nation equals mother equals soil (62). The film itself complicates the trope at the same time as it entrenches it in the cinematic idiom of the late twentieth century in India. Mishra contends that the term Mother India "has hegemonic privilege and presence" in Indian culture because of the symbolic meaning it holds in several Indian languages[4] (Mishra 68). Thus for Mishra the term carries within itself,

> ...echoes of the very loaded Hindi *bharat mata* ("mother India"), the softer, poetic Urdu *madre hind*, the more autochthonous Sanskrit compound *matrbhumi* ("mother earth") as well as Bankim Chandra's famous nationalist song *Bande Mataram* ("I bow to you, Mother"). (Mishra 68)

In this listing of the title "Mother India's" linguistic connotations, Mishra shows how deeply the film and its main character, resonated, and continues to resonate, with the consumers of Bollywood. The director's choice of the English title "Mother India" as opposed to the Urdu *"madre hind"* or the Hindi *"bharat mata"* signals the director's attempt to appeal to the largest possible viewing audience, regardless of the audience's location.

Furthermore, since the film opens with establishing shots of the land with the song *dharati mata* (mother earth) playing in the soundtrack, the audience is left with no doubt as to the actual subject of the film (68). Thus, the film's representation of motherhood and womanhood encapsulates within it the equation of mother with the land, as well as with the ultimate sustainer, nurturer and goddess figure, whose wrath, once evoked, cannot be escaped easily. What is clear in this depiction, however, is that "Mother India" (and by extension the nation India) is an imagined construct, one that is distinctly Hindu, and intrinsically tied to the "land" itself.

This particular representation of "mother" is also asexual—mother cannot be imagined as having a sexual life. As pointed out earlier, Radha remains husband-less for the latter half of the film. Rosie Thomas goes so far as to describe her as a destroyer of men. As Thomas points out, "she is both venerator of men and venerated by them as *devi* (goddess) and *maa* (mother), and she is, in turn, in need of men's protection and a protector and destroyer of men" (16). Even though *Mother India* opens with images of Radha as bride, wife, farmer (who coaxes even the most barren land to produce crop) and then mother of sons and an entire village, her own needs and desires as a sexual individual are curiously silenced and elided in the film, a trend that was to dominate Hindi cinema for decades. This ties in to the importance and deep-rooted symbolism of the figure of "mother" in Indian culture, the mythology of which does not include sexual desire, and instead, envisions "mother" as supremely chaste, honourable and admirable for her power derived from her chastity.

As Vijay Mishra shows, the figure of "mother" in India is not just a nurturer, a sustainer, or even just "mother earth" but the carrier and transmitter of "culture," in itself a loaded word. We are all familiar with the argument that it is the mother's responsibility to "teach" and to educate the offspring, along with fulfilling the role of the nurturer. *Mother India*, with its multi-layered depiction of the fierce goddess-like "mother" reinforces that particular ideology. As Edward Said shows, in his discussion of images and cultural artifacts, cultures use their cultural forms to represent themselves[5] (16) and Bollywood cinema sees itself as the key forum/art form through which India is represented and, I would argue, even constructed. According to Mishra, Bollywood is "self-consciously about representing, in the context of a multicultural and multiethnic India, the various disaggregated strands of the nation-state—political, social, cultural, and so on" (65). In its representation of "mother," *Mother India* has taken the biggest idea in the land—the symbology and cultural significance of the mother figure—and turned it into the most significant symbolic statement on Indianness (Mishra 65).

I began with the image of the self-sacrificing, almost asexual, non-individualistic image encapsulated within Nargis's portrayal of "Mother India" and I move now to the 2006 movie *Pyar Mein Twist*, which presents a very different "mother." Situated in cosmopolitan Mumbai, focusing on the elite, educated and rich upper-class, the movie *Pyar Mein Twist* shares very little with the iconic *Mother India*. It is, quite literally, a comparison of apples to oranges, and I therefore proceed with caution here. *Pyar Mein Twist* revolves around a love affair, but as the title indicates (Twist in a Love Story), the love affair is not the traditional boy-meets-girl story. It portrays two elderly people widowed and lonely after the demise of their respective spouses, who meet, fall in love and conduct an affair publicly, much to the embarrassment of their adult children.

In every sense of the word, the movie is the complete opposite of *Mother India*. Where the setting in *Mother India* was rural, in *Pyar Mein Twist,* it is urban. Where the driving force in the former was abject poverty, in the latter it is extreme affluence complete with "foreign" cars and dinners in expensive restaurants. Where the mother inspired undying love and gratitude from her sons in *Mother India,* in *Pyar Mein Twist* she is subject to complaints and recriminations for causing social embarrassment. In *Pyar Mein Twist*, the jean-clad Dimple Kapadia (the actress portraying the protagonist Sheetal) looks elegant, youthful and well-cared for as opposed to the sari-clad and sun-burned[6] Nargis in *Mother India*. Commercially, the film was a modest success, nowhere near the resounding success of *Mother India*.

As Tejaswini Ganti shows, films like *Pyar Mein Twist* are now considered worth investing in, due to the largely globalized audience. Indian theatres traditionally seated anywhere from 1000-2000 people, but with the advent of multiplex theatres in urban centers and a global market, that seat a smaller number of people in a theatre, investors see adequate return on "smaller budget, off-beat films focusing on elite, urban lifestyles produced for limited release" (Ganti 65). Given Bollywood's investment in the representation and construction of a specific type of Indian identity, in the new transnational and global arena, Bollywood's significance has increased manifold. While discussing the portrayal of parents in Hindi films of the 1990s, Meheli Sen shows that the Bollywood film industry actively expanded its viewing audience to include diasporic audiences. According to Sen, to generate foreign revenue, Bollywood had to "revamp itself to compete as an equal in the global marketplace of images, and [...] the diasporic citizen had to be interpolated as an 'Indian' subject within the filmic fantasy" (148). In spite of its melodramatic, and obviously constructed, representation of "reality" Bollywood now functions as the connection to the homeland, the "motherland," bringing with it its unique version of what it means to be "Indian."

The mother character presented in the film *Pyar Mein Twist* is one who is completely devoted to her family, and one who has sacrificed most of her personal life in order to run the family business and to provide for her two daughters. Her "sacrifice" is honoured and acknowledged within the film, but she is continuously exhorted by her peers to permit herself to finally make a life for herself. The storyline does not dwell on the fact that Sheetal refused to marry after her husband's death, and focused on expanding his business and raising her two daughters. Instead, the movie opens with the chance meeting between Sheetal and Yash, both of whom have recently decided to "retire" from their respective businesses and relax a little. They decide to explore their feelings for each other, but are discovered by their children, all of whom oppose the romance vehemently. Interestingly, their friends and peers encourage them to continue exploring their romance, going so far as to provide them with a hidden cottage and a secret vacation. The movie ends with a dramatic confrontation between the sets of children, resolved by a monologue from Yash. The setting of the movie, the costumes as well as the storyline, all seem to address an audience that may not necessarily be the Indian "masses" and instead addresses a new "urban" audience, one that has exposure to more sophisticated themes and settings. It also pays tribute, in part, to Bollywood's diasporic audience, one that may not necessarily buy into the specifically "Indian" sacrificial mother presented by *Mother India*.

The film, however, continues to present a sacrificial mother, if not necessarily an abjectly sacrificial one—Sheetal is a mother of daughters not sons, and is about to "lose" her daughter to marriage. The threat of a lonely, isolated life looms large on the horizon for Sheetal, and her only salvation now seems to be a second marriage. Even when she runs away with Yash, she defers to his plans, plays the demure beloved, and is defended and spoken for by Yash when attacked by her daughter and Yash's children. "Mother" in this film is represented as a strong individual woman, one who can hold her own in the business and social milieu of urban India but one who is still willing to sacrifice her new love affair for the sake of her younger daughter's happiness. I refer to the moment in the film in which her daughter's prospective mother-in-law threatens to break off her daughter's engagement because of the rumours circulating around Sheetal's personal conduct. It is Yash who insists on continuing the romance, and persuades her to elope with him, helping her realize that she is, and was, a desirable woman before she was a mother.

Arguably, *Pyar Mein Twist* begins where *Mother India* leaves off. *Mother India* shows Nargis as a content, gracefully aging grandmother who has fulfilled all her life's prescribed roles—bride, wife, mother, leader and grandmother—satisfactorily. *Pyar Mein Twist*, on the other hand, focuses on the looming threat of a lonely life, spent without the love and support of a man—even if that man is a loving son—and neutralizes that

171

threat by introducing Yash's character. The film even includes an aging sister-in-law, Ms. Arya, played by Farida Jalal, who strongly encourages Sheetal to pursue her romance, using her own loneliness and dependency as an example. Ms. Arya, in fact, becomes instrumental in re-uniting Sheetal with Yash after Sheetal decides to give up her romance so that her daughter's engagement can continue.

The question here, then, is not whether all mothers are portrayed as self-sacrificing nurturers, but whether mothers who only have daughters, no sons and no husbands, can continue to live a fulfilled life. Can it be said that only mothers of sons can age gracefully into doting grandmother-hood without the benefit of husbands? Sheetal, for example, lacks male support and thus needs to marry, even if that marriage comes late in life. Not only does Sheetal need a man to support her in her old age, she has to learn to defer to his wishes and to his control over the relationship after decades of remaining independent. The ease with which she plays the role of the demure, shy partner in the courtship is troubling. The film manages to challenge the nation-mother-soil equation set up by *Mother India*, but continues to portray mothers as an odd combination of strength and servility, as well as power (when it comes to decisions about the home and the family) and the lack of it when dealing with the "significant other."

Bollywood has tried recently, in films like *Pyar Mein Twist*, to "update" the figure of the mother as presented by Nargis's portrayal of Radha, and to make her a woman with a career and a life of independence and freedom. And yet Bollywood cannot move away from the traditional view of the mother as the "ideal" homemaker. Strength, individuality, even sexuality are highly valued, but always with a caveat. Strength must be combined with a certain level of deference, individuality must be sacrificed for the greater good and sexuality must be reined in and controlled by social dictates. Both Sheetal and Radha actually have a lot more in common than my paper has suggested so far. Both sacrifice themselves for their children, both are successful "career women" who take over their husbands' roles successfully (Radha's farming and the family business for Sheetal) when necessary, and both raise children without feeling the need for a husband. Radha, however, can continue to live on her own even after the marriage of her son precisely because she is the proud mother of a son and the mother of the village, while Sheetal must marry, because she can only be a threat and a burden on society after her daughter marries and leaves her home. It is one thing to live as a widow with a young child in tow, and quite another to enjoy life alone after the daughter is married.

Although completely different in their historical contexts and their portrayals of motherhood, both films share the highly-valued ideal of the self-sacrificing mother. Given the intrinsic investment of audiences in the mother-equals-soil-equals-nation equation, the representation of "mother" in both films embodies the nurturing and compassionate mother-figure, one who willingly sacrifices her own desires and needs in order to raise "good" citizens. In both films, women are respected, even honoured, for their strength and resilience as single mothers, as mothers who can successfully raise their children and feed and clothe them without a husband's help. In as much as the portrayals are intrinsically troubling (mothers do not have sexual needs or desires in both films), the representation of the mother-figure in Bollywood seems to be undergoing a change, as Bollywood begins to re-vamp itself to cater to the demands of an increasingly cosmopolitan audience. However, as the portrayal of motherhood in *Pyar Mein Twist* has shown, mothers cannot put their own needs and desires before the needs of their children. The role of "good mother" as portrayed by Nargis and Dimple Kapadia, is in direct conflict with the role of "desirable, sexy woman." The perfect mother remains one who is the perfect home-builder, and the perfect nurturer, which automatically precludes any other role.

ENDNOTES

[1]Cinema in India has a complex history. Bollywood, or Hindi Cinema, is India's largest film industry, based in Mumbai. It dominates the film industry in India, but there are other film industries, some of which produce films in regional languages. This paper will focus on Bollywood's representation of India in Hindi films.

[2]The words "*laaj*" and "*izzat*" are generally translated into English as honour, but bear deeper connotations in both Hindi (*laaj*) and Urdu (*izzat*). When referring to a woman's honour, the words imply sexual purity, virginity and innocence. According to Vijay Mishra, both words "are so culturally specific that the English gloss fails to capture their cultural resonances" (70).

[3]Hinduism is a Polytheistic religion, based on a complex pantheon of

gods, goddesses (*devas* and *devis*) and their offspring, all of whom are representations and aspects of a single divine energy that is nameless and has no form.

[4]Mishra's account of the three different words for mother in the three major languages of India evokes the political complexities that mark the interactions of these languages. During, and after, the British rule, languages were divided along religio-ethnic lines—the Sanskrit-based Hindi was claimed as the language of the Hindus and the Arabic-Persian based Urdu became the language of the Muslims. Bollywood films consistently mark subtle differences in language—Muslim characters invariably use Urdu words and diction. When spoken, both Hindi and Urdu share enough words to make conversations possible. Scripts, however, are completely different. For details, see Gould.

[5]In the first part of his book, *Culture and Imperialism*, Said argues that nations have found it beneficial to draw distinguishing borders between cultures as well as to "invent" historical traditions that legitimate imperial power and domination (15-19) a legitimation that has occurred through cultural forms like literature, art, and more recently, through film.

[6]Sun-burned and darker skinned women in the Indian context are not considered to be beautiful or desirable. Sun-burned skin indicates exposure to the sun, which in turn associates the woman with the lower castes, who spend most of their time tilling land or completing other menial tasks in the urban setting (sweeping streets, etc). A woman belonging to the upper-castes would not spend her time outdoors, and would, instead, be well taken care of.

WORKS CITED

Ganti, Tejaswini. *Bollywood: A Guidebook to Popular Hindi Cinema*. New York: Routledge, 2004. Print.

Gould, William. *Hindu Nationalism and the Language of Politics in Late Colonial India*. Cambridge, UK: Cambridge University Press, 2004.

Mishra, Vijay. "The Texts of 'Mother India'." *Bollywood Cinema: Temples of Desire*. New York: Routledge, 2002. 61-88. Print.

Mother India. Dir. Mehboob Khan. Perf. Nargis and Raj Kapoor. 1957. DVD.

Pyar Mein Twist. Dir. Hriday Shetty. Perf. Dimple Kapadia and Rishi Kapoor. 2005. DVD.

Roy, Parama. "Figuring Mother India: the Case of Nargis." *The Bollywood Reader*. Eds Rajinder Dudrah and Jignah Desai. New York: Open University Press, 2008. 109-121. Print.

Said, Edward. *Culture and Imperialism*. New York: Vintage Book, 1994, Print.

Sen, Meheli. "'It's All About Loving Your Parents': Liberalization, Hindutva and Bollywood's New Fathers." *Bollywood and Globalization: Indian Popular Cinema, Nation, and Diaspora*. Eds. Rini Bhattacharya Mehta and Rajeshwari V. Pandharipande. New York: Anthem Press, 2010. 145-168. Print.

Thomas, Rosie. "Sanctity and Scandal: The Mythologization of Mother India." *Quarterly Review of Film & Video* 11 (1989): 11-30. Print.

Baburao Bagul's *Mother*

A Case of "Outlaw" Dalit Mothering

MANTRA ROY

IN *JANANI: MOTHERS, DAUGHTERS, MOTHERHOOD*, editor Rinki Bhattacharya outlines the importance of motherhood in India when she writes: "Indian societ(y) condemn(s) ...women who fail to give birth to children" and "childless women are routinely ill-treated as inauspicious creatures" (26). This ideology of motherhood presumes that women will be sacrificial, loyal, devoted and fulfilled in their role as a mother and will perform their motherly "duty without rights or rewards" (Bhattacharya 26). While this patriarchal ideology can have negative repercussions for all Indian women, it is particularly harmful for Dalit[1] women, who have historically been subjugated within Indian society (Kapoor). In this chapter, I undertake a close textual analysis of the work of Baburao Bagul, one of the most eminent Marathi Dalit writers of the twentieth century. I focus on his short story "Mother" to examine how a widowed Dalit mother's agency and "outlaw mothering" become compromised, trapped as she is in the nexus of caste, class, and patriarchy. In the sections that follow, I will first provide some context on the Dalit community in India, and then provide an analysis of the story, showing how it represents a case of "outlaw" mothering, with a critical reflection on representing the subaltern mother.

DALITS AND DALIT WOMEN

An understanding of the historical circumstances in which Dalits have endured life in India brings clarity to why the expression of agency by the Dalit mother in Bagul's work is a courageous, potentially life threatening act. In the past, Dalits were referred to as "untouchables." This term emerged from the four-fold caste system in India that has been in practice for thousands of years. This hierarchy designated a section of people as "untouchables" or "outcastes" of society who did not belong to the caste structure. The "untouchables" were responsible for disposing of dead bodies, working with carcasses of animals and their hides for leather, cleaning the toilets, and keeping the neighborhoods germ and disease free. Ironically, the outcastes received the title of "untouchables" because they touched and dealt with the filth and pollution of the entire society.

Social interaction with upper castes, including eating together, sitting next to each other, going to the temple or school, living in the same neighborhoods, friendships or marriage, was strictly prohibited. "Untouchables" were relegated to the outskirts of society, denied access to education, temples, employment outside their ancestral professions (which were often unhygienic), and public social interactions in market places. Crossing the boundaries and social codes demarcated by the caste system was dangerous because higher castes, having more wealth, resources, and social status carefully guarded their positions in Indian society. Dalits were regularly beaten or killed for trespassing these social codes. Economic and social disempowerment has thus characterized their lives in most parts of India (Kapoor).

For women, the situation was and continues to be more complex. Due to poverty, most Dalit women have to work outside the home. In rural areas, they join their husbands and other men in agricultural work, and in urban and semi-urban areas, Dalit women earn livelihoods through menial work or low-paying strenuous labor. On these worksites, many Dalit women become sexually exploited by the upper caste men who are their employers (Benegal 1974; Devi 2002). These men do not deem them to be untouchable when it comes to sexual advances, rather they assume that due to their outcaste status they should be sexually available and accessible.

This subjugation of a Dalit woman's body is further reinforced by Dalit men in her own community. Scholars have used the term "Sanskritization" which refers to a practice among some lower caste groups to adopt Brahmanical[2] cultural codes—which restrict women's mobility and sexuality—in their attempt to attain higher social status (Deshpande; SarDesai). As a result, even though Dalit women have to earn a living, they are often condemned for leaving the home-space to work, and regarded as promiscuous by Dalit men (Franco et al. 72).

Back in the domestic sphere, Dalit women are expected to fulfill their duties as subservient wives and dutiful mothers. The contradictions Dalit women encounter—the pressure to support the family economically, the fear of sexual exploitation by employers, and the family's suspicion and dismissal of them as promiscuous—inform their maternal identities. In spite of these challenges, they are expected to be good, loving, self-sacrificing mothers who should be devoted to their children's welfare and nourishment at all times. The confluence of poverty, caste and patriarchy impose challenges on Dalit mothers governing their decisions, sexuality, and sense of self as seen in the story "Mother."

SUMMARY OF "MOTHER"

In "Mother," Baburao Bagul ponders over what happens if a Dalit mother deviates from the ideology of womanhood and motherhood that is imposed upon her by attempting to assert her independence after the death of her husband. While this story has a tragic ending, it illustrates the agency that a Dalit mother embraces to rise above her circumstantial restrictions, albeit briefly.

Pandu's mother is an attractive widow who lives with her ten-year-old son, Pandu, in a semi-urban "untouchable quarter" (Bagul 184). Rather than living the life of an asexual widow who is dependent on her community for support—as is expected of her after her husband's death—she chooses to earn her own livelihood and enter into a sexual relationship. This is a brave decision, because as a Dalit widow she is in a highly marginalized position in Indian society, as well as within her own Dalit community.

The story begins with Pandu's classmates accusing his mother of being a "whore" and sleeping with the *mukadam* (overseer) (Bagul 183). Humiliated but defensive about his widowed mother, Pandu returns home to find cockroaches in the bread basket and putrid food in vessels. Now he ponders the recent changes in his mother—the new sarees, the new silver chain, the self-adoration in front of her mirror, and not sitting with him during dinner or speaking to him before going to work—and begins to find evidence of his mother's love-life. As Pandu begins to weep loudly, his neighbors hear him and begin hurling abuses at his absent mother for prioritizing her sexual needs over her mothering duties.

At that moment Pandu's mother is rushing back home to cook for her son; seeing the crowd at her doorstep she realizes Pandu "[has] turned against her, joined the enemy ranks" (Bagul 186). Noticing the "suspicion in [Pandu's] eyes" she sees a replica of her tuberculosis-ridden, decrepit, and jealous husband from ten years ago. While she labored all day at work on construction sites to earn money to sustain the family, her physical beauty convinced her husband that she "sold her beauty for a price" (Bagul 187). He subjected her body to indecent examination every night to feed his conviction about her supposed adulterous life (187). The more his health failed and the more he became frustrated with his "joblessness" the more he became violent with his wife. Complete lack of trust and disrespect for the hard work she did to support the family made Pandu's mother desperately lonely, helpless, and, eventually, fiercely aggressive.

Now, ten years later, when she finds Pandu eyeing her with similar suspicion, her "love....concern for [Pandu] slowly [turns] to rage" and the "full force of her fury" unleashes itself: "Die, you bastard! Like your father who died of his own evil" (Bagul 188). While Pandu childishly concludes "his mother [does]not need him anymore" the mother immediately relents her harsh words and realizes that "ever since she had met the overseer, ...she had neglected [Pandu]..." (Bagul 189). She tries to pacify him with new clothes she has bought for him, but Pandu, "disgusted at the thought of his classmates jeering at him" and convinced that his mother "[has] really gone to the bad now," shouts at his mother: "Whore! I spit on your clothes..." (Bagul 189). Pandu runs out of the house and his mother stands rejected—"[h]er pain [knows] no bounds" after having lived these ten years since her husband's death only for Pandu (Bagul 189). She has refused several suitors only to love and care for her son.

In the final scene in the book, the mother is crying late into the night when a knock on the door ushers in hope for her that Pandu has returned. But she opens the door to find her overseer-lover. While the overseer initiates lovemaking, another light knock on the door is indeed from Pandu. But the overseer's lust and "bear-like hug" do not allow the mother to reach out to her weeping son who, having witnessed his mother closely intertwined with the "towering figure of the overseer," is devastated and runs out into the street, his "fast falling tears almost [blinding] him" while dogs snap at him (190). The book ends with the mother left in this heartbreaking predicament as she unsuccessfully tries to escape from her lover's arms in order to embrace her son.

OUTLAW MOTHERING

In *Mother Outlaws*, Andrea O'Reilly discusses how "patriarchal culture" deems those women "'bad' mothers" who "resist patriarchal motherhood and achieve empowered mothering" (2). In other words, women who do not subscribe to selfless sacrifice, unquestioned devotion to children, and complete self-effacement, become "outlaws"' from the institution of motherhood as defined and imposed by patriarchy (O'Reilly 2). However, what happens to the mother who dares to parent her child on her own terms but whose agency is silenced by the forces that delimit her subaltern life? Can she be a successful outlaw mother? What happens to the mother who perhaps wants to be a 'good' mother to her children but her powerless position in society overwhelms her mothering? Baburao Bagul, in representing a silenced but extraordinary mother, attempts to articulate the impossible space inhabited by the subaltern mother as she tries to be a 'good' mother to her child. He demonstrates how the 'bad mother' status of Pandu's mother emanates from her insistence on parenting her child on her own terms. The torrent of abuse her community hurls at her and Pandu's rejection of her makes her sacrifices invisible. By bearing witness Bagul makes the subaltern's agency, mothering on her own terms, 'speak' in spite of its erasure by her son and community's condemnation.

Through the jealous, now dead, husband of Pandu's mother Bagul depicts the repressive patriarchy that blames its failures on the woman while putting the woman through unbearable emotional and physical tortures. Bagul indicates that because the Dalit man cannot earn the household income after his illness and has to rely on his wife, he feels doubly emasculated. Outside the domestic space he is crippled by his caste identity and now inside the domestic sphere, his gender prerogative of being the provider is compromised owing to his failing health. Pandu's father abuses his wife physically and aims to destroy her beauty which sharply contrasts with, and seems to augment, his own sense of helplessness owing to "his disease, his failing strength, his joblessness" (Bagul 187). These nightmarish experiences traumatize Pandu's mother for life because her manual labor at construction sites and her monetary income are not good enough evidences of her dedication as a wife and mother. Bagul portrays the predicament of a subaltern woman who is forced to rise above her gendered role of a submissive and male-dependent entity because of her partner's inabilities; but she is condemned for her transgression.

Bagul highlights another aspect of the subaltern woman's plight. After her husband's death, Pandu's mother continues to be victimized by the men in her community who lust for her and view her independence as a challenge to their male prerogatives. The drunk Dagdu tries to rape and molest her and when readers meet her for the first time, Bagul writes "[t]he men [strip] her bare in their mind's eye" (Bagul 186). The women find her husband-less status and her physical appeal threatening to their conjugal lives and direct their condemnation of her by focusing on her non-conformist mothering. Moreover, her affair with an upper class and upper-caste man, the overseer, makes the community treat her as a whore. The community blames her because it cannot accept a low-caste, poor but beautiful widow fending for herself and her son without seeking help of other men and women. Also, because patriarchy has created the ideology of motherhood in order to control female sexuality, the spectre of the mother-figure as a sexual being threatens and disrupts gender discourse (Franco et al. 32). Pandu's mother emerges as a "bad mother" who challenges the notions of patriarchal motherhood and does not forgo her personal sexual pleasures. She refuses to compromise her self-hood while being a committed mother. While her neighbors condemn her as a whore, she ignores them because if her body can fetch security for her child, she will not hesitate to utilize it for his sake. As an empowered mother, incorporating "agency, autonomy, authenticity, and authority," she becomes what O'Reilly calls an "'outlaw' mother" (O'Reilly 11). However, when Pandu begins to reject her, she is shattered and her agency is cut short and silenced. Pandu is too young and inexperienced to realize that his mother strikes a balance between challenging the oppressive ideology of motherhood and raising him on her own terms.

When his mother arrives at the scene of his neighbors cursing her at her doorstep, only Pandu views her with his "new-found knowledge" and observes her "tightly-worn sari, the careless confidence, the defiance in her walk" and considers her lips "reddened...with betel juice" as "evil" (186-7). Pandu is now "convinced of her guilt" and he is prepared to "take sides against her" (187). Bagul reveals the complex network of pressures Pandu's mother encounters here: the community judges her as a failed mother and uses this as a weapon against her, and her son in his innocence cannot understand her *own* way of loving him.

When Pandu's mother confronts Pandu and his "glance that [takes] her in from top to toe," she remembers the "accusations" her "TB-ridden, suspicious, nagging" husband had hurled against her during his ailing life. Pandu, still a child needing his mother's love and care, understandably misjudges her wrath and does not understand that these words bear venom not against him but against society. Because his mother in all her frustration seems so alien to him at this point, Pandu, employing his child's logic, decides for himself that his mother "[has] murdered his father and [will] murder him" (188). I posit that Bagul emphasizes the flow of criticism Pandu's mother has to encounter only because she is an unconventional mother who fulfills her maternal duties in a non-conformist way. She notices his "thin, spindly arms… concave stomach…and the whitish pallor of his skin" and shudders at the thought of losing him to TB like his father. Her intensive mothering reasserts itself when she worries about Pandu's health, "'Have you been coughing? … do you feel feverish? Don't be stubborn, tell mother'" (188). However, soon the mother feels guilty about having "neglected him [her son] … [not] even touch[ing] him" as she [is] overwhelmed by her lover's "strong arms" to which she surrender[s] gladly after ten years of "loneliness" (189).

Because Pandu's mother begins to retreat into the ideology of motherhood, she feels guilty for having neglected her son in favor of her lover. Realizing her lack of attention to Pandu and feeling remorse for shouting at him in anger, she apologizes to him: "'Son, forgive me…I've brought you some new clothes…come eat, son. Forgive me, I'm just … old [and] silly'" (189). This is where the subaltern Dalit mother re-inscribes the code of ideal motherhood and dismisses empowered mothering. The ideology of motherhood is so deep-seated that the mother condemns herself as a failure when she recognizes her transgression of prescribed codes. The agency she exercises to parent her child differently is wiped out when she begins to view herself as a "bad" mother.

A mother who lived ten years of her life as a widow, forever tormented by men around her, "only for [Pandu]" and "tried so hard to love" him finds her world crumbling around her when that son becomes an accomplice of the community and accuses her of being a whore and abandons her. "[C]rying helplessly" she recalls all the men who [have] tortured her, including her husband, the neighbors, and now her son (189). Bagul reveals the sacrifices she makes only for her son: how she

"could have lived a merry life" with either of the men who offered to marry her, like Mohammed Maistry who offered her a
car in exchange of marriage, Walji Seth who tried to bribe her
to become his mistress, and Dagdu who wanted to surrender
his life's savings to her. But she refused all of them and "gave
up everything...." (190)

The mother's complete devotion to Pandu's well-being becomes articulated when she confesses, "'I lived for you, hoping you'd grow up,
be my support, but you have betrayed me...'" (190). The price she pays
for her nonconformity defeats her strength and agency. While she fights
against the community whenever they berate her son for her supposed
"business," she crumbles under the weight of her son's disparagement,
misunderstanding, and rejection (189). Through these circumstances,
I argue, Bagul demonstrates the consequences Dalit outlaw-mothers
encounter when they try to exercise agency as well as the circumstances
that stifle their non-conformity.

REPRESENTING THE SUBALTERN MOTHER

An important critical concern about depicting subalterns pertains to the
intellectual's responsibility in re-presenting them. Gayatri Spivak suggests the position of the investigator needs to be questioned because the
intellectual should engage with speaking to, and not for, the historically
muted subject of the subaltern woman and should not essentialize her
(Spivak 295). Bagul writes Pandu's mother's story because it needs to
be told. A Dalit subaltern mother suffers multiple lines of repression
and Bagul's "Mother" represents the impossibility of meeting these
demands. It is intriguing that Pandu's mother has no name or identity
except in terms of her relationship with Pandu, reminding us of Adrienne Rich's description of the ideology of motherhood as requiring the
absence of selfhood for the mother. Consequently, the breach of that
relationship leaves Pandu's mother with no social identity in a society
hostile to the claims of a subaltern woman's sexual independence and
refusal to adhere to prescribed codes of motherhood. Ultimately, the
subaltern mother cannot enact her agency, or, symbolically "speak." It
is Bagul, who, in tracing Pandu's mother's narrative, speaks for her and
her agency that would not be otherwise archived because she herself

surrenders to the pressures of dominant ideologies. We may recall that in charting the agenda of the subaltern historians, Priyamvada Gopal writes that Subalternists take the responsibility to articulate or "speak" for the silenced subaltern (140).

Although the subaltern mother attempts to exercise agency in her own way, she is rendered invisible by the social norms and expectations of her community. Spivak notes that there "is no space from which the sexed subaltern can speak," and Bagul attempts to retrieve, re-create and re-present this silenced mother's extraordinary mothering that is otherwise subsumed in the noise of social criticism (307). Bagul, in the mode of subaltern historians "[bends] closer to the ground" to re-cover the "residuum" of a silenced subaltern experience (Gopal 140). Spivak warns both postcolonial intellectuals and subaltern historians against essentializing the subaltern experience when speaking for the subaltern woman. Bagul does not adore Pandu's mother, nor does he censure her for her non-conformist mothering. Rather, he explicates the multiple lines of repression the subaltern woman has to negotiate to prove herself as what is deemed a "good" mother by her social milieu. While it may be argued that Pandu's mother's subversion of patriarchy is temporary, it is a story that needs to be told, even though it is told to us by a man. It is an important depiction of the resistant subaltern consciousness in praxis.

ENDNOTES

[1]The fifth category of the caste system in India, the untouchables or outcasts, is today known as Dalit (literally, broken down or oppressed). The term "Dalit" was first used in 1873 by Jyotirao Phule, one of the first social justice activists to challenge the dehumanization of the un-touchables in the nineteenth century. "Untouchable" is a rarely used term today.

[2]Brahmanism refers to religious, social, and cultural codes ordained and preserved by Brahmins, the uppermost caste in the Indian caste system. These include practices such as maintaining caste purity through endogamous marriage and monitoring and regulating women's sexu-ality. Upper caste women were assigned a ritual high status, including less mobility outside the home, which has often been equated with the "Indianness" of these women.

WORKS CITED

Bagul, Baburao. "Mother." *Poisoned Bread.* Ed. Arjun Dangle. Bombay: Orient Longman, 1992. 183-190. Print.

Benegal, Shyam, dir. *Ankur.* Blaze Film Enterprises, 1974. Film.

Bhattacharya, Rinki, ed. *Janani: Mothers, Daughters, Motherhood.* New Delhi: Sage Publications India Pvt. Ltd., 2006. Print.

Deshpande, Ashwini. "Casting off Servitude: Assessing Caste and Gender Inequality in India." *Feminism and Antiracism: International Struggles for Justice.* Eds. France Winddance Twine and Kathleen M. Blee. New York University Press, 2001. 328-348. Print.

Devi, Mahasweta. "Shanichari." *Outcast: Four Stories.* Trans. Sarmistha Dutta Gupta. Calcutta: Seagull Books, 2002. Print.

Franco, Fernando, Jyotsna Macwan, and Suguna Ramanathan, eds. *The Silken Swing: The Cultural Universe of Dalit Women.* India: Sangam Books Ltd., 2000. Print.

Gopal, Priyamvada. "Reading Subaltern History." *The Cambridge Companion to Postcolonial Literary Studies.* Ed. Neil Lazarus. New York: Cambridge University Press, 2004. 139-161. Print.

Kapoor, S. D. *Dalits and African Americans: A Study in Comparison.* New Delhi: Kalpaz Publications, 2004. Print.

O'Reilly, Andrea *Mother Outlaws: Theories and Practices of Empowered Mothering.* Toronto: Women's Press, 2004. Print.

Rich, Adrienne. *Of Woman Born: Motherhood as Experience and Institution.* New York and London: W.W. Norton & Company, 1986. Print.

SarDesai, D. R. *India: The Definitive History.* Boulder, CO: Westview Press, 2008. Print.

Spivak, Gayatri Chakravorty. "Can the Subaltern Speak?" *Marxism and the Interpretation of Culture.* Eds. Nelson, Cary and Lawrence Grossberg. Urbana: University of Illinois Press, 1988. 271-313. Print.

Contributor Biographies

Amber Fatima Riaz completed her Ph.D. program in English at the University of Western Ontario in 2012 and is currently teaching Reason and Writing at Fanshawe College in London, Ontario. She has presented conference papers on the representation of mothers in film, and published an essay on parent-activists in New York in the Demeter Press Anthology: *The 21ˢᵗ Century Motherhood Movement*. She has also published essays on the Partition of India, and on the representation of the "burqa" in Tehmina Durrani's novel, *Blasphemy*. Her dissertation on the representation of the Muslim Veil in Pakistani Literature is entitled: "Architectures of the Veil: The Representation of the Veil in Pakistani Feminists' Texts." Her research interests include Postcolonial studies, Feminist literary theory and South Asian Studies, as well as the intersections of diaspora, religion and migration in South Asian Literature in English.

Amrita Pande is a lecturer in the Sociology department at University of Cape Town, South Africa. Her research primarily focuses on globalization, gendered bodies and gendered work spaces, new reproductive technologies and new forms of social movements. Her work has appeared in *Signs: Journal of Women in Culture and Society, Qualitative Sociology, Feminist Studies, Indian Journal of Gender Studies, Reproductive Bio Medicine*, and in several edited volumes. She is currently writing a monograph based on her multi-year ethnography of surrogacy clinics in India. She is also involved as a performer and educator in a theatre production, *Notes from a baby farm*, based on her work on surrogacy. Her other ongoing projects include research and advocacy work on the sponsorship system of migration and its effects on the lived experiences of migrant domestic workers in Lebanon.

Baldev Mutta has been in the field of social work for over years. He is the Founder and CEO of Punjabi Community Health Services (PCHS). He has worked for the last 20 years developing an integrated holistic model to address substance abuse, mental health and family violence in the South Asian community. He has used an asset-based community development approach to develop parenting programs in the Punjabi community. These parenting programs are run in partnership with religious institutions and school boards. He has received many community awards for his work on equity, community development, diversity management, and organizational change. He has his own television show, *Community ConneXion*, which is aired every Saturday on channel 851, Rogers Cable (this is a specialty channel).

Jasjit K. Sangha completed her Ph.D. from OISE/University of Toronto in the Department of Adult Education and Community Development. She has been working on issues related to mothering for nearly a decade, exploring how women engage in transformative adult learning through the process of (step) mothering. She is the author of the book, *Stepmothering: A Spiritual Journey* (2012) available through Demeter Press, and has also published in journals such as *Qualitative Inquiry*, *Women and Environments* and *The Canadian Journal for the Study of Adult Education*.

Lynne Lohfeld is an Associate Professor (part-time) at McMaster University's Department of Clinical Epidemiology and Biostatistics. She has developed and taught undergraduate and graduate courses in qualitative research, and led research on immigrant and women's health issues, as well as on palliative care, knowledge uptake by health care practitioners, and improving the quality of services and outcomes for long-term care facility residents. She has a Ph.D. in medical anthropology, an M.S. degree in rural sociology and an MPH degree in international health. Currently she is a consultant on an NIH-funded project with members of Johns Hopkins Bloomberg School of Public Health to develop and implement innovative ways to reduce the impact of malaria in parts of Zambia and Zimbabwe.

Manavi Handa is a registered midwife in Ontario and Assistant Professor at Ryerson University. Raised by parents who immigrated from India in the mid-1960s, she grew up surrounded by discussions of racism, assimilation and cultural retention. As a midwife, Manavi has focused her practice on marginalized women, with a large proportion of her clients being new immigrants from South Asia.

Mandeep Kaur Mucina is currently working towards a Ph.D. in the Adult Education and Community Development program at OISE and finished a Master's degree in Social Work, from the University of Toronto. Mandeep has been active in the South Asian community, as a community based educator as well as providing therapeutic support to South Asian communities around issues of Violence Against Women (VAW) and family violence. Mandeep's Ph.D. research focuses on second-generation South Asian women and their experiences of honour-related violence, particularly exploring how second-generation South Asian women in Canada negotiate cultural knowledges, such as izzat or "honour" and exploring women's experiences of family violence that emerges from "honour."

Mantra Roy's research interests include caste, race, ethnicity, gender, and broadly, postcolonial studies. The politics of representation in different media, including visual culture, has also been Roy's focus. South Asian, particularly Indian, literature and cinema are Roy's current areas of research. Roy's dissertation was a comparative study of representation of subalternity in India and the United States. She is currently enrolled in a Nonfiction Writing Certificate program at the University of Washington.

Rachana Johri is an Associate Professor of Psychology at Ambedkar University, New Delhi, India. Her doctoral thesis entitled "Cultural Conceptualization of Maternal Attachment: The Case of the Girl Child" was an analysis of the intersection of culture and gender in the experience of mothering daughters in a culture marked by son preference. Apart from motherhood, she has written on the use of narratives in research on women, particularly in the Indian context. Her other major research interests include violence against women and gender, disability and mental health.

Sadia Zaman is Director, Original Program Development, CBC News and Centres. Before her move to CBC, Sadia was the Executive Director of

Women in Film and Television – Toronto, a high profile not-for-profit. Sadia has spent her entire career in the screen-based industry and held many leadership positions. She is also an award-winning writer, producer, host and interviewer who has created hundreds of hours of television at public service broadcasters Vision TV, TVO, and CBC. Sadia's work has been nominated for three Gemini awards. Shows she worked on won another two Geminis. In 2007 she was also a finalist for the Atkinson Fellowship in Public Policy. She has been named a trailblazer and was one of four Canadian journalists awarded a prestigious Southam Fellowship for Journalists in 1998.

Satwinder Bains is an instructor at the University of the Fraser Valley and the Director of the Centre for Indo Canadian Studies. Her research interests and expertise include Indo Canadian Cultural Studies, identity politics, migration, settlement and citizenship, diaspora studies, multi-lingual and cross-cultural education. Satwinder has over 27 years of work experience in community development and has worked extensively with women, youth and families from the South Asian community.

Seema Kohli is an artist based out of New Delhi, India. Her works reveal a claiming of feminine subjectivities, an altered concept of feminine sexuality. Her works bring into focus a woman's physical attributes, her intellect, thoughts, dreams and realities. The domain of sacred feminine geography with an effulgence of energy emanates from the paintings, where myth, memory and imagination have become the handmaiden of her own artistic oeuvre. Within the genres of sexuality and desire, one can't ignore the parallel journeys of discovery that she has made. Being a student of philosophy, she has inhaled and experienced myriad notions of existence, and has lived emotional and psychological reality. For more information please see <www.seemakohli.com>.

Soumia Meiyappan is a Research Associate with the Family Health Team at the Toronto Western Hospital. This position has allowed her to work on projects and programs that respond to the specific health needs of the local community, including: improving primary care access for recently immigrated young women and their children; an initiative aimed at helping patients manage their diabetes; evaluating the effectiveness of a home-based care program for elderly patients; and quality improvement of care. She holds a Masters degree in Health Research Methodology from McMaster University and her thesis was focused on the first-time motherhood experiences of Tamil immigrant and refugee women living in Toronto. Her research interests include qualitative research approaches, immigrant and refugee women's health, new motherhood, and community-based research approaches.

Srabani Maitra is an Adjunct lecturer in the Department of Women's Studies at the University of Waterloo and the Coordinator for a SSHRC-funded project at York University. She completed her Ph.D. in Adult Education from OISE at University of Toronto and was a SSHRC Post-Doctoral Fellow in the Department of Equity Studies at York University. Her research examines the efficacy of the various training and learning programs created by the Canadian government in facilitating professional immigrant women of colour's entry into the Canadian labour market. Her other areas of specialization include transnational service work, migration, enclave entrepreneurship and the South Asian diaspora.

Tahira Gonsalves has completed studies in Sociology in India and Canada. Her research and policy work span the areas of international development, social and economic policy for women, and the immigrant and mental health sectors in Canada. She has worked at the International Development Research Centre and at the Canadian Research Institute for the Advancement of Women, in Ottawa. At present she works for the Ontario provincial government.

Tarnjit Kaur has a doctorate in Physics. She has worked as a research scientist for ten years and has authored and co-authored over 30 peer-reviewed research publications. Currently Tarnjit lives in Ottawa with her partner and two young children and is taking a career break. She writes for on-line independent media on subjects as varied as the occupation of Iraq, energy policy and Sikh feminism. She has given educational presentations on sex selective foeticide, green building design, and urban micro-generation of wind and solar energy.

Acknowledgements

From Jasjit:

I would like to thank Demeter Press and especially Andrea O'Reilly for her ongoing support of my work, and for making it possible for this book to go from an idea I was conceptualizing, to an actual publication. Thank you to Luciana Ricciutelli for her wonderful work with the layout.

Thank you to all of the contributors to this collection for bringing forth important work on South Asian mothering, as well as for their patience and dedication throughout the process of developing this book. Thank you to Tahira Gonsalves for coming on board at the right time and helping to bring this project to life, while also juggling a busy work and family schedule.

Thank you to the Centre for Women's Studies in Education at OISE/ University of Toronto for lending me a great space to work in, and in particular to Jamie Ryckman, Angela Lytle and Lorena Gajardo for listening when I needed to chat and validating the importance of this project. A special thank you to Roxana Ng (1951-2013), a pioneering feminist scholar, for her encouragement and mentorship over the past decade.

Thank to you to Roland Sintos Coloma, Kenneth Huynh, Shaista Justin, Bikram Dhillon and Sukhjeet Dhillon for providing me with insightful feedback on early drafts of this work.

Thank you to Bina Mittal, Sadia Zaman, Misbah Mukri, Rizvana Talreja and Zainab Moghal for our ongoing conversations about South Asian mothering and for providing me with a space to discuss my ideas. Thank you to Claudia Faleiro and Tania Janthur for reminding me to take time out for some fun.

Thank you to my parents, Harbans and Balvinder, and my sisters

Satvir, Karamjit and Benita for their unwavering belief in me and for caring about this work. Thank you to Kami, Kael, Kamaya, Amitoz, Harjeevan, Jaan, Adeola, Jada, Alanda, Sheena, Danuszia, Rosa and Jericho for keeping me grounded as I worked steadily on this project. And finally, a big thank you to my husband, Robin, and my children, Simryn and Zeulewan, for cheering me on from the sidelines and being an absolute delight to be with.

From Tahira:

I would like to thank Eric for his never-ending understanding and support throughout this process and, a future thank you to Safik, for when he is old enough to understand why I worked on a book on mothering, instead of doing my actual mothering! I would like to thank Jasjit and other friends who are mothers, for the inspiration they provide me. And most of all, I would like to thank my own mother, Madhuri, who taught me how to mother in so many ways with her deep love and support.